JUST THE PLAGUE

JUST THE PLAGUE

Ludmila Ulitskaya

Translated from the Russian by
Polly Gannon

GRANTA

Granta Publications, 12 Addison Avenue, London W11 4QR

First published in Great Britain by Granta Books, 2021

Published by arrangement with ELKOST Intl. Literary Agency

First published in Russian as *Просто чума*
in 2020 by AST, Moscow

A CIP catalogue record for this book is
available from the British Library.

2   4   6   8   9   7   5   3   1

ISBN 978 1 78378 805 7
eISBN 978 1 78378 806 4

www.granta.com

Typeset in Bembo by Patty Rennie

Printed and bound by CPI Group (UK) Ltd,
Croydon, CR0 4YY

When I was forty-five, I wrote a screenplay called *The Plague*. I was hoping to be accepted onto Valery Fried's scriptwriting course. My application was rejected. Thirty-two years have passed, and the script has now acquired a new significance.

1988–2020

Contents

Translator's Note

TRANSLATING AND TRANSLITERATING Russian names into English is not a matter that can be decided once and for all. Of course, there are several codified systems of transliteration that are widely adopted and applied in academic texts, but these are often not appropriate for texts meant for a wider readership. Naming practices in Russian and in English differ fundamentally, and in many ways. For a Russian speaker, English naming practices often seem excessively simple, almost denuded of meaningful information. Russian names, on the other hand, carry levels of contextual nuance and meaning that an English speaker cannot hope to grasp immediately, and that the English language cannot easily accommodate. For every name in English, there are three or four in Russian – all designating the same person. Thus, anglophone readers often assume there are far more characters than there actually are in any given Russian text. And when a text, or screenplay, does in fact boast a multitudinous cast, a translator might be inclined to throw up her hands in despair. In this text, for example, Tonya Sorin (whose last name, in Russian, takes the feminine form 'Sorina') is called, depending on the situation and the speaker, either 'Tonya' or 'Antonina Platonovna'. She might also be called 'Tonechka' or 'Ton' (though in this text she is not). Where she is designated as 'Antonina Platonovna', reflecting the more formal speaking situation between her and Dr Sikorsky, I have called her, simply, 'Nurse Sorin'.

In this translation, I have tried to streamline the Russian system as far as I could, anglicizing (transliterating) the names without straying too far beyond a framework recognizable to a Russian speaker. Some translators substitute English names for Russian – i.e., Andrew for Andrei – but I have chosen not to do so. My practice has been to preserve the names and patronymics, but to use informal nicknames (which in English sound just like 'ordinary' names) more consistently than they would be used in Russian. I have also regularized surnames, in some cases, so that the feminine marker is absent (i.e., Esinsky, not Esinskaya, for the wife of Esinsky; Sorin, not Sorina, for the wife of Dr Sorin).

I want to avoid, if at all possible, a jolt of estrangement in the middle of reading the text, which can be disastrous to narrative momentum – that moment of hesitation when the reader thinks, for example: 'Wait, who was that again?

Is Antonina Platonovna the same person as Tonya?' or, 'Is Vera Esinskaya related to Konstantin Esinsky?' An anglophone reader wouldn't automatically make the connection between the two names, and certainly wouldn't automatically assume that Vera Esinskaya is Esinsky's wife.

The Russian title of this book, *Просто чума* ('Just the/a Plague'), has an added layer of meaning that is impossible to convey in English, but is important nonetheless. 'Just a plague!' is a colloquial expression that means something along the lines of 'it was crazy!' or 'holy-moly!' in English. These expressions register amused surprise more than anything else. And it's the same with 'just a plague!'. It can also have a negative implication – but not a very profound one. Say your bathroom gets flooded when the bath overflows – 'just a plague!' you might say (usually when you're retelling the event), thus making light of a bad situation. This colloquialism adds another layer of (rather playful) irony to the title, which otherwise suggests something ominous and tragic; which, indeed, it is.

Translation is a form of 'deep reading', a kind of oscillation in which the translator occupies a place between. This is an uneasy space to dwell in – at times one feels pulled apart in all directions. Working on this text, however, has been more like communing at once with Ludmila Ulitskaya; Alex Klimin, the editor of the Russian text; and

Sigrid Rausing, the editor of the English text. At the best moments, everything (and everyone) has come together in what felt like a curious, always collaborative, linguistic dance. All the dance needs to complete it is a reading audience, out there in the world, and eventually in some as yet unimaginable 'posterity'. In that sense, it is a dance always open to the future.

Cast of Characters
(in order of appearance)

GALYA — Tatar woman, porter at the Anti-Plague research centre

RUDOLF IVANOVICH MAIER — Research scientist at the Anti-Plague research centre, who accidentally infects himself

ANNA ANATOLIEVNA KILIM — Maier's lover, mother of his child

MASHA — Maier's wife, incapacitated by a stroke eight years ago

LUDMILA IGNATIEVNA KOSTRIKINA — Woman train passenger

SEMYON KULKOV — Train passenger, agriculture student who breeds geese

SVERBEEV — Train passenger with lopsided face*

---

* Translator's note: It is not specified who or what Sverbeev, the Lopsided man, is, but he is clearly a mildly unsavoury character, perhaps a petty NKVD operative or undercover agent, since all he has to do is show his ID to get what he wants at the telegraph office.

| ZINKA | Woman train conductor |
| ELENA DMITRIEVNA | Old woman train passenger wearing worn-out boots |

THE ZHURKINS:

| IDA GRIGORIEVNA ZHURKIN, NÉE SOLYUS | Staunch Party loyalist; daughter of famous Bolshevik |
| ALEXEI IVANOVICH ZHURKIN | Member of the board of the People's Commissariat of Public Health, known as Narkomzdrav. Less fanatical than his wife |

THE GOLDINS:

ILYA MIKHAILOVICH GOLDIN	Head of the Moscow Autopsy Institute and chief pathologist
SONYA ISAKOVNA	His wife
NASTYA	Their housekeeper

THE ESINSKYS:

| KONSTANTIN ALEXANDROVICH (KOSTYA) ESINSKY | Member of the board of the Commissariat of Public Health |
| VERA ANATOLIEVNA | His wife |

The Esinskys share a small partitioned flat with their daughter and son-in-law, a common arrangement during that era of state-mandated communal housing.

THE PAVLYUKS:

COLONEL PAVLYUK — NKVD officer, member of the board of the Commissariat of Public Health

NATALYA (NATASHA) — His wife

THE SORINS:

ALEXANDER MATVEEVICH SORIN — Admitting physician in the accident and emergency department of Ekaterininskaya Hospital

TONYA — His wife, a nurse at the same hospital

RECEPTIONIST at Hotel Moscow

TATIANA DMITRIEVNA SOZONOVA (TANYA) — Chambermaid

ANADURDYEVA — A People's Deputy from Turkmenistan, stays at the Hotel Moscow and encounters Maier at the reception desk

LORA IVANOVNA MAIER — (on telephone) Maier's sister

YAKOV STEPANOVICH	NKVD Commissar of Public Health, organizes the search and enforced quarantine of those possibly exposed to the plague
PETROVICH	Hospital porter
VERY HIGH PERSONAGE, second only to the Big Boss (Stalin)	

THE PETROVSKYS:

FEDYA AND HIS WIFE	Ordinary family whose daughter has already fallen victim to the regime
KOLYA, KLAVA AND VERKA	Friends of Semyon Kulkov, the young agriculture student on the train
IVAN LUKYANOVICH KOZELKOV	Train crew chief, Kazan railway station in Moscow
CAPTAIN SOLENOV	NKVD officer
FEDOR VASILIEVICH	NKVD officer, suffers a heart attack on the job
OLYA	His secretary*

---

* Translator's note: originally named 'Galya', like the old Tatar woman, the porter, at the beginning of the text, and renamed to avoid confusion.

JUST THE PLAGUE

ACROSS VAST WASTES of snow, a freight train makes its way, its headlights cutting through a maelstrom of swirling white flakes. It moves slowly, deliberately. It passes a city buried in snowdrifts, barely visible under layers of white. The city dissolves in the snowy gloom.

A long, one-storey building sits at the edge of this world sunk in snow. Dim lights burn in a few of its windows. The name on the sign, powdered in white, is illegible.

The porter, an old Tatar woman, a kerchief pulled low over her forehead with a large headscarf on top of it, sits at a table next to an iron stove. She slices pieces of dried meat with a little knife and chews them toothlessly. Her gaze is concentrated, but devoid of thought.

Rudolf Ivanovich Maier is in the laboratory clean room. He wears protective gear – a suit and a mask. His face is invisible. Gloves cover his hands. With a long needle, he disperses cultures in Petri dishes. A spirit lamp burns, the flame swaying with the smooth, precise, mesmerizing movements of his hands.

The telephone on the table in front of the porter starts ringing. It is loud and insistent. The old woman is in no hurry to pick up the receiver.

'Keep at it, screeching like the devil,' she grumbles. The telephone refuses to be pacified. She picks up the receiver.

'Laboratory! It's night-time! It's already night, I said! What are you so worked up about? There's no one here. No, I can't write, no. Maier? He's here. Hang on. I said hang on!'

The old woman disappears into the depths of the corridor, knocks on the furthest door, and shouts:

'Maier! Telephone! Moscow calling! Get the phone!'

She tugs on the door, but it's locked. She knocks harder, and shouts:

'Maier! Come out! The chief is calling, he's mad!'

In the clean room, Maier puts down the needle, and goes still. The knocking agitates him.

'I'm coming, I'm coming!' His voice is muffled underneath the mask. The mask shifts slightly, the sealing ring comes loose and slips below his chin.

The woman hears him, and goes back to the telephone:
'Hang on, he says . . .'

In the anteroom, Maier removes the gloves, the mask,

4

the protective suit, carefully wipes his face and hands, and rushes out to grab the phone.

'I'm sorry to keep you, I was in the clean room. Right, nocturnal experiments. Vsevolod Alexandrovich, I'm not ready. In principle, yes. Absolute certainty. But I still need a month and a half, or two. Yes, a month and a half. But I'm still not ready to report the findings . . . Well, if you put the matter like that. But consider the report preliminary. I absolve myself of responsibility. All right, goodbye then.'

He hangs up the phone, clearly annoyed. The old woman looks at Maier attentively:

'At me, they shout. At you, they shout. That devil of a chief is mad as a hornet. Here, have something to eat!' She extends the knife with a piece of dried meat on it. Maier waves her off.

'No, thank you, Galya,' he says, but takes the morsel anyway, and starts chewing mechanically.

'Go home and get some sleep. Go home! Why are you still up and about?'

Dawn has not yet broken, the windows are dark. There is a cautious ring of the doorbell. A young woman lights a small lamp, gets up without a sound, and walks to the door. A child is asleep.

Rudolf Maier has come to see his secret girlfriend, Anna

5

Anatolievna Kilim. He is still wearing his snow-covered sheepskin coat, though he has taken off his hat.

'Has something happened?' Anna asks, blinking in fright. Rudolf unbuttons his coat.

'Nothing in particular. They called me to Moscow tonight. To report to the board. The work isn't finished yet. It's ridiculous. But they never take no for an answer. They want it here and now. I'm going, Anna. I just came to tell you.'

'Straight away?'

'Tonight. I stopped the experiment. There's something I need to do before I go.'

'Who will stay with Masha?'

'I've already arranged it. Savielova will stay with her for a week.'

'How is she doing?'

'The same. She sits in her armchair, staring into space . . .'

Anna presses her palm against Rudolf's cheek, moves it to his forehead.

'Do you want to come to Moscow with me? For a few days?'

'Right now? How can I?' Anna says, taken by surprise.

A little face peeps over the edge of the bed, beams when she sees Rudolf, and is crawling up onto his lap in no time.

'So, our little Krosya has woken up, has she?' He strokes her curly head. 'Ask Maria Afanasievna to stay overnight with Krosya, and we'll be on our way.'

'But I can't leave just like that. I really can't. Right now we're on the school break, but even so I have things to do at school.'

'Ask them to let you go, to postpone your duties for a bit. You can think of something, can't you?'

'I'll try, Rudy. You know how much I'd like to go with you.'

'Send me a telegram at the Hotel Moscow when I'm there, and I'll meet you, how about that?'

There are four of them in the compartment. Rudolf Maier sits next to the sliding door by the aisle, his sheepskin coat draped over his shoulders. Next to him, in front of the fold-out table, sits Sverbeev, a sturdy man with a hard face that looks somehow lopsided. Opposite the man Ludmila Ignatievna Kostrikina, a pretty woman with plaits piled high on her head, heavily made-up and smartly dressed, is laying food out on the tiny table. Across from Maier is a young man, Semyon Kulkov, provincial in appearance, but lively and talkative.

'Now, that's better. I like it when everything is nice and pretty. Nowadays no one knows how to set the table, but I

7

like it when everything is in its right place – forks, knives, and plates, with proper napkins,' Ludmila Ignatievna Kostrikina says, admiring her evenly cut pieces of sausage resting neatly on slices of bread. Sverbeev, the man with the lopsided face, watches her with great interest. Semyon Kulkov returns to his previous topic.

'So, as I was saying, Ludmila Ignatievna, I wrote a letter and I'm waiting to see whether or not they'll answer it. He's an academician, after all! At our agricultural school they're a bunch of deadbeats – we get no support from them, nothing . . .'

'Go ahead, have something to eat,' Ludmila Ignatievna says to the others, and Sveerbev takes a sandwich. Still wrapped up in his story, Semyon Kulkov also reaches out his hand. He continues talking.

'So I decided to act on my own, at my own risk. I took them and started to raise them in my own barn, to tame them and get them used to cold, little by little. The third generation is coming up already. Frost-resistant. I held a talk, and everyone seemed to ridicule me for it. That's when I decided to write a letter. I kid you not. Straight to the Academy of Sciences. Within two weeks the invitation arrived. So I packed up and left – I'm on my way now. We're all like that in my family. Once we set our sights on something, there's no going back.'

Maier shivers, hunching his shoulders. Kulkov turns to address him:

'Excuse me, what field are you in, if you don't mind my asking?'

'Me? I'm a doctor.'

'That's good. That's good. So you can grasp a biological idea – the succession of positive traits through breeding . . . proper breeding, that is to say.'

'*Weeell*,' Rudolf says, drawing out the word. 'I'm a microbiologist, you see. I'm afraid my object of study obeys different laws.'

'What do you mean, different? How are they different?' Kulkov says, getting a bit heated. 'We all live according to one law, Marxist–Leninist law!'

'Here, come on now, have something to eat,' the Kostrikina woman urges, rather flustered.

'Naturally, that goes without saying,' Maier responds earnestly. 'Only my microbes don't know that.'

'In this day and age everyone should know that!' the young man continues vehemently. 'Last year, the mean temperature in February was twenty-nine below. And my geese survived it perfectly. The barn is made of plywood too – it might as well be made of air. So if we perform the experiment, let's say, on cattle, if we can breed frost-resistant livestock, we could do away with cattle barns.

Imagine the advantages that would have for our Soviet nation.'

The sliding door opens, and Zinka, the conductor, pokes her head in.

'I'm putting an old woman in here with you, she's standing in the corridor. Do you mind? She'll only be travelling for four hours.'

'Sure, we can make room!' Semyon Kulkov moves to free up some space, and the old woman, Elena Dmitrievna, squeezes in with her bundles.

'May I ask for some tea?' Maier says to the conductor.

'Tea? At this time of night? You'll have to wait till morning. Teatime is over,' the conductor says gruffly.

They begin getting ready for bed. Maier sleeps on the top bunk. Sverbeev settles underneath him, after removing his fur-lined travelling boots. The old woman, drawing up her legs in their big, worn-out, lace-up boots, curls up in the corner at his feet. Semyon Kulkov goes out to the corridor.

At the end of the corridor, in the vestibule, is a cage with two geese in it. He bends down and puts a piece of wet bread into the cage, waking up the birds. They stick out their necks, and he strokes them.

'Good boy, good boy. We're going to the Academy, yes we are!' he says, patting a thick white neck.

Maier wraps himself up in the light travel blanket and puts his fur hat on. Sverbeev asks Ludmila Ignatievna quietly:

'Are you from Moscow yourself?'

'Yes, born and bred. I've lived on Lesnaya Street from birth.'

'Lesnaya? Where is that?'

'By Belorussky Station.'

'Ah, I know, I know. Well, maybe you'll invite me over for a visit sometime?'

'Goodness me, we've hardly met, and already you want to pay a visit . . .'

'I'd come over and we could get to know each other better. Just give me your address.'

The old woman eyes Sverbeev's fur-lined boots, standing on the floor right in front of her. Fine boots.

And again, the train moves through the vast wastes of snow. The steady beam of the headlights pierces the darkness, illuminating a single, unchanging stretch of snow and wind, snowdrifts, and more snowdrifts . . .

The conductor opens the door of the compartment, proffering a glass of tea.

'Hey, someone was asking for tea. Was it here?'

Everyone else is still asleep. Rudolf Maier leans down from the top bunk and takes the tea.

'Thank you. Thank you very much.'

'No problem.'

The conductor leaves. She goes to the stove at the end of the aisle, washes glasses. The door between the corridor and the vestibule is slightly ajar. The passengers wake up. The train slows down.

'Oh, could you go outside for a just minute, please? I need to get dressed,' Ludmila Ignatievna says.

Sverbeev wakes up, and rummages around on the floor for his boots. They aren't there. The old woman is gone too. But her worn-out old women's boots, with laces, are still there.

'She pinched them! That old granny pinched them!' Semyon Kulkov announces gaily.

'What do you mean, pinched them?' the former owner of the boots says. 'How could she? I'll fix her, see if I don't! Give me your boots, so I can go out to the station,' he says to Kulkov.

'How can I give them to you? I need to wear them myself!'

'Well, who would have thought! Who would have thought . . .' Ludmila Ignatievna says, suppressing laughter.

'Pardon me, but are you going outside? How about letting me wear your boots? I've got to go out to the station,' the injured party says in a wheedling tone to Maier, who frowns, and questions him.

'What exactly is the matter?'

'See, that old woman stole my boots. I need to go to the station and call someone to have her detained,' Sverbeev says hotly.

'All right, wear mine then,' Maier acquiesces, and his fellow bunker stuffs his feet into the boots.

The telegraph department of the railway station. Sverbeev wrenches the door open.

'What do you think you're doing? You can't come in here!' the telegraph operator shouts.

Sverbeev pulls out his ID, thrusts it in front of her face, and she desists. He sits down.

'Put me through to . . .'

And again the train – trundling through the cosy, familiar central Russian terrain – the train is already nearing Moscow.

Moscow. Kazan Station. People tumble out of the train carriage. Maier, looking downcast, shuffles on his way. The crowd thins out. The only person left on the platform by the train is a young fellow with a cage containing two geese, frozen solid. Semyon Kulkov crouches by the cage and whispers:

'But why? What happened? It wasn't all that cold, was it?'

Tears run down his healthy red cheeks.

Morning at the home of the Zhurkins. A bare round table, with a frying pan on it. Daily life strongly marked by the ethos of Communist austerity. Ida Zhurkin, a plain, un-adorned, but striking woman with a penetrating gaze, puts aside her newspaper and says to her husband:

'No, Alexei, no. You never met them. But I knew them! What people they were! Courageous, fearless, tal-ented! They were my father's friends, and the last years of his life – he was bedridden – they visited him con-stantly. And I knew them, I knew them all. I loved them, admired them. I couldn't understand them, naturally, I was a child then, very young. Even my father couldn't under-stand them. And he had an extraordinary mind – a mind of honesty, fortitude; well, you know yourself what a man he was. But they all became degenerates! Every last one! I cried over their speeches, and then, later, over their trials. Beyond belief! But there was some flaw, some fatal incon-sistency – the Intelligentsia didn't accept the Party all the

14

way. They backed off. Degenerated. And the terrible roots they put down, they have to be dug out and burned to ashes. Otherwise the Revolution will perish!'

Alexei Ivanovich listens attentively, scraping the frying pan with his fork to get the last of the potatoes.

'You're right, of course, I have no objections,' he says quietly.

Ida opens the newspaper under her elbow and begins scouring it.

'It's here somewhere ... wait a moment.' She combs through the pages, but can't find what she's looking for. Alexei glances at his watch.

'Time for me to go, Ida. I'll be back late tonight. I have a board meeting,' he says, getting up from the table. The newspaper rustles as Ida continues her search for what interests her, to no avail.

Professor Goldin's apartment. Silverware, plates and cups for breakfast, eggs on a serving dish, jam in a bowl, are all laid out on a tray – everything is very European, if not quite *ancien régime*. Nastya, the housekeeper, a neat, middle-aged woman, carries the tray to the dining room, and puts it down. She knocks on a door leading to another room, and shouts:

'Ilya Mikhailovich! Breakfast is ready!'

The door opens and Ilya Mikhailovich Goldin comes out – a tall, solidly built man, no longer young. He appears to be rather sombre.

'Thank you, Nastya.'

He shouts:

'Sonya! Why are you dawdling?'

Ilya Mikhailovich looks through the newspaper. His wife Sonya comes in – grey-haired, attractive, slender.

'I was first, as usual,' he says, adding, 'Where is Lena?'

'Lena left early today. There's a problem with her lab work, it seems.'

'Very poor education, as far as I can judge, very poor,' he says in a stern voice.

'Do you mean to say that in Vienna they get a better education?' his wife asks acerbically, tipping them into their own private banter.

'Well, just a tiny bit. But maybe I'm imagining it.'

'Ah! Ilya Mikhailovich! It appears that you display too much admiration for bourgeois science! When I was studying at the Sorbonne, the pedagogical process was very imperfectly monitored! Can you imagine that the trade union organizers even failed to keep an attendance list of the students?!'

'What an outrage! *C'est impossible!*'

*

A single room divided by a partition. In bed, the Esinskys, a married couple. They are about fifty, but Vera Anatolievna doesn't show her age. Her face looks young, bright, and lively. She puts her lips close to her husband's ear and says:

'Kostya, are they asleep?'

Konstantin Alexandrovich listens.

'I think they are.'

'No, I hear some sort of movement over there. Shhh!'

On the other side of the partition is a very young couple, in bed. The young husband asks his wife in a whisper:

'What do you think, are they sleeping?'

'What else would they be doing?' the still-girlish wife responds, over his shoulder.

Vera Anatolievna whispers to her husband behind her palm:

'How uncivilized it is to live like this, in one room with one's own grown-up daughter!'

'That's for sure,' her husband whispers back, and embraces her. 'I'll be away until the day after tomorrow. I have a board meeting this evening, and I go to the station to catch the night train directly afterwards.'

'You won't come home first?'

'No, I won't have time. In Leningrad I have to be present at a dissertation defence. I'll take the night train back.'

Then they fall quiet, hearing a soft giggling behind the partition.

Colonel Pavlyuk is standing by the window. His face is strong, with regular features. A military bearing. Without turning round, he says to his wife:

'Natasha, I'll take breakfast with me.'

'And you won't be coming home for lunch?'

'I can't.'

'The whole day without a meal again? Your ulcer will open up, Sergei,' Natasha says, wrapping up the sandwiches. 'Maybe you'll be able to get away after all?'

'No, I won't,' he says laconically.

A car engine rumbles downstairs in the street.

'Time to go.'

The apartment door slams shut. The lift door slams shut. He's gone. His wife shakes her head.

Tonya Sorin stands by the mirror. She plaits a thick hair extension into her own hair. Her husband, Alexander Matveevich Sorin, watches her darkly. His gaze is heavy with suppressed agitation.

'Everything about you, Tonya, is false. Even your hair.'

'You've just noticed?'

'No, I saw it long ago. The first time I saw your false plait on the pillow, I nearly died of disgust.'

'Well, you didn't, did you? Because here you are.'

'Lies! From the very beginning, it was all lies, all lies!' Alexander Matveevich grimaces. 'Remember what you said at the Brynovys', when we first met? Remember?'

Tonya stuffs some hairpins into her mouth and says through pursed lips:

'Why should I remember? You have a good memory – you tell me.'

'I do remember. I remember how you lied, saying you were a doctor. A neurologist, to be precise.'

'A good nurse is no worse than a doctor. If you don't like nurses, I can leave. Right now.'

'Where will you go? Where?' Alexander Matveevich says hopelessly, and with contempt.

'I'll find somewhere. I'll go back to where I came from,' Tonya throws out carelessly. 'Hey, maybe I'll even prefer my own company, since my husband's foul temper gets worse every day.'

'I know where you'll go. You'll be a streetwalker.'

'It's none of your business where I go!' Tonya looks into the mirror with satisfaction. Her hair has turned out beautifully – luxuriant, upswept tresses.

'You're a vacuous feather-brain, Tonya. Incapable of

anything at all. You can't even make a pot of soup, or bring home a loaf of bread . . .'

'Well, as soon as you get to your office, you can send Dusya out to fetch it. Or Alka. They do anything you ask, with pleasure . . .' Tonya smiles insolently.

'All right, let's go. We'll be late.' Alexander Matveevich pushes away his cup and gets up from the empty table.

'You go ahead, I'll find my own way,' Tonya snaps, and turns to the mirror again.

Alexander Matveevich leaves the house, slamming the door behind him.

In the Hotel Moscow, a chambermaid is standing by the receptionist's desk.

'I walk into the room, and I can't believe my eyes! Just imagine. The mattress cover is on the floor, along with all the bedclothes – those are on the floor too.'

'Really?' says the receptionist in wonder.

Maier, in his snow-covered hat and sheepskin coat, waits at the desk for them to notice him. But they pay no attention and continue their conversation.

'Really! The mattress cover right on top of the rug, and the blanket, pillow, and everything else on the floor too . . .'

'You've got to be joking, Tanya . . .'

'Well, apparently she's used to sleeping on the floor.'

The chambermaid sniggers.

'A People's Deputy she may be, but she's still uncivilized.'

'What do you expect, that they'll change as soon as they receive a medal?'

'Pardon me,' Maier says, interrupting them. 'I have a reservation. The name is Maier.'

The receptionist rummages through her papers with displeasure.

'Here it is. Room thirty-six. Passport, please,' she says without lifting her head, and peers at the document.

At the end of the corridor, a Turkmen woman appears. Tall, slender, decked in heavy silver bracelets, earrings, and rings. On her striped silk dress – a jumble of dull silver and carnelian – medals, various pins, an Order of Lenin, a bunch of clinking, bright metal. She approaches the desk. She stops, and smiles politely. Her eyebrows are arched, her eyes long and narrow, high cheekbones, full lips – a beauty. Maier looks at her with interest. She smiles shyly.

'I feel the cold coming off you,' she says, wrapping her shawl more snugly about her shoulders.

'Can't do anything about it – that's our climate,' Maier says, smiling, scrutinizing this Eastern rarity.

'I'm going home, to Ashkhabad. It's warm there,' she replies. And, turning her long neck and facing the receptionist, she says, almost peremptorily:

'Take my key, please.'

And leaves. The receptionist and the chambermaid are discomfited.

'Hmph. Royalty. And she still sleeps on the floor!' is all the chambermaid can say.

Maier takes his passport and the key to the room, and strolls down the corridor, smiling.

The room is small. Maier looks around, takes off his coat, and rubs his freezing hands. He dials a number on the phone.

'Lora! I'm here in town for a few days. I came to give a report. No, no, I'm staying at the Hotel Moscow. Yes, I'll be sure to stop over. I'm frozen stiff. I'm afraid I caught cold. No, I'll come by, it's been so long. I have a favour to ask. Anna may come tomorrow. Will you put her up for a few days? Alone, alone, without our daughter. What are you talking about, Lora? Masha's still the same. Stares out the window at nothing, hardly eats at all. No, she can't walk. In an armchair. I put her to bed at night. She doesn't have any more seizures. My dear, you're mistaken, it's been eight years already, not five. Well, all right, till tomorrow then.'

He looks at himself in the mirror. Runs his hand over his cheek – he needs a shave. He goes out into the corridor, and asks the chambermaid:

'Could you tell me whether there's a barber in the hotel?'

'Sure. On the first floor.'

Maier glances at his watch, and hurries to the lift.

Reflection in the mirror. A barber's hands deftly manipulating a straight razor above Maier's cheek. The barber's voice:

'Another ten minutes and I would have been gone. You're lucky.'

Maier coughs, wants to cover his mouth, but he is wrapped in a sheet. The barber pats him on the shoulder and lifts up the razor.

'Go ahead, cough for all you're worth.'

Maier says apologetically:

'I seem to have caught cold on the train. I sat in a draught.'

The barber wipes down the blade till it gleams.

'Some people are surprised that I still use a straight razor blade. They don't realize that the shave is closer, cleaner. And that it simply looks better. Lift your chin, please. Just like that.'

Maier throws his head back, and the barber touches the blade to his neck. Suddenly, Maier breaks out in a hacking cough. The barber has no time to move his hand away, and a tiny red line appears on Maier's neck.

'Good lord!' the barber exclaims. 'This is a first for me. You jerked your head, that's why!'

He sprinkles eau de cologne on a napkin and hastily presses it against the wound.

'Don't worry!' Maier says, reassuring him. 'I started coughing . . .'

'Just a moment! I have some alcohol too. It disinfects better than the cologne. Just a moment.'

'Never mind. It's nothing at all, please don't worry about it,' Maier says.

'Nothing, you say!' The barber is beside himself with worry. 'It has never happened to me before, that someone passing through my hands ends up in this condition. If only you knew who I have shaved in my time – you wouldn't believe it! I worked at the Kremlin!'

He points at the sky.

'With this very razor! Everyone knows me. I'm Kotikov. Veniamin Alexeevich Kotikov!'

Blood trickles from the cut. The barber rushes around, removes one napkin from the cut, and replaces it with another one.

Maier smiles.

'Why are you so upset, Veniamin Alexeevich? I always shave with a safety razor at home. I'd cut myself every day if I used a thing like that. Calm down, please, everything's all right.'

Meeting of the board of the Narkomzdrav, the Commissariat of Public Health. Eight of the top brass are listening attentively to the report. One is wearing a military uniform. This is Colonel Pavlyuk, from the NKVD. Maier is concluding his talk.

'Now, as you can see, it is clear that the choice of this highly virulent strain was completely justified. And although the study, from my point of view, has still not been carried out to the end, it is essentially complete. Soon, we will have the first samples of a new vaccine at our disposal. It is effective against all known strains of the plague.'

Esinsky asks a question:

'Tell me, if you would, Rudolf Ivanovich, how long do you expect it will take to move the vaccine into production, and how difficult is the technology of production likely to be?'

Maier rubs his temples as though he has a hard time grasping the sense of the question. It seems to be more than he can cope with.

'In order to finally . . . We need around a month and a half to be absolutely sure of the preparation. Around three months will be required for testing, then production of a sample batch; and the rest doesn't depend on me. Or, rather, it depends on the financing of production, on its organization. Technology . . . in terms of technology, nothing fundamentally new will be required, apart from enhanced safety and security measures.'

Grigoriev, the chairman of the board, looks at his watch.

'Comrades! Today we are here on a matter of exceptional significance; an event, I would say, with significance for all humanity. The development of a vaccine is one more step towards the full victory of Communism throughout the world, one more proof of the triumph of Comrade Stalin's policies. We congratulate Rudolf Ivanovich. Thank you for your work, for your report. I would request that you come to see me at two o'clock. We will have to work out a plan.'

The members of the board begin to stir, then relax, and slowly start to disperse.

Esinsky goes up to Maier.

'Rudy! Congratulations! Brilliant work.'

Maier just rubs his eyes and says nothing.

'What's wrong, are you tired?'

'More than you can imagine.'

Colonel Pavlyuk approaches Grigoriev, chairman of the board.

'Vsevolod Alexandrovich, we'll be having a conversation

about this work. I think it needs to be transferred to our agency.* Think about it. For the time being, the plan should be halted.'

Grigoriev gives an understanding nod.

Esinsky looks at Maier again.

'What's wrong with you, Rudolf? Should I call a car?'

'I seem to have caught cold on the train. I'm afraid I may be coming down with pneumonia. That's how these things always end with me,' Maier says, forming the words with difficulty.

'Wait, I'll call for a car to take you back. Where are you staying?'

A car rolls up to the presidium of the Academy of Medical Sciences on Solyanka. Esinsky settles Maier in the back of the vehicle and waves his hand.

'Get better, Rudolf! Call me the day after tomorrow. I'll be back from Leningrad, and I'll come by to see you. Great work, by golly!'

'Thank you, Kostya.'

Anna Kilim sits on the train bound for Moscow with an intelligent-looking older woman. There are glasses of tea

---

* The NKVD was the state security agency under Stalin.

on the fold-out table. The compartment is cosy, dimly lit. Anna speaks.

'Never in my life have I travelled like this, in a private compartment! When I was on my way to the station, I already had such a holiday feeling! And then I see you! Elena Braslavskaya! What a surprise. Mama told me so much about you. She even showed me the house your pharmacy was in.'

'It was on Dvoryanskaya Street,' says the older woman, almost in a whisper.

'Yes, now it's called Gogol Street!

'You know, Elena Yakovlevna,' Anna adds, 'I still have Mama's treasure box made of Karelian birch, where she used to store her correspondence, and there are many letters in it from you.'

'I gave that box to her on her sixteenth birthday. The twelfth of May, 1910.'

'Yes, that was Mama's birthday! And you remember it ...'

'I remember everything, child. Every single thing. How we went to the skating rink, and how we were invited to our first ball, and how we both fell sick with scarlet fever on the very same day – and then we both returned to our lycée on the same day too, and we cried with joy! We had an extraordinarily happy childhood. It was full of fun, full of music. Your mother was so musical. Exceptionally so!'

'Yes. But her career as a performer didn't take off. She worked as a teacher all her life, and she began teaching me from an early age. I'm also a music teacher, Elena Yakovlevna,' Anna says, smiling.

'You resemble your mother, Anna. The more I look at you, the more similarities I can see.'

'Mama said that you parted ways even before the Revolution, before the war. She thought you were living in Bulgaria . . . or was it France?'

'No, it wasn't like that at all. Before the war, my husband and I moved to Persia. He was a diplomat, in the Czar's foreign service. Then we lived in Constantinople. During the Revolution we returned to Russia. My husband was one of a small number of diplomats who took up service in the new government. My parents did emigrate, though. I haven't heard from them in a very long time. I doubt that they are still alive. I don't know whether my husband is alive, either. He . . . well, he was sent into exile, without the right to correspond . . . Everyone, I lost everyone.' Elena Yakovlevna is talking calmly, almost without emotion. 'How ironic that only five years ago your mother was still alive, and I knew nothing about her . . . Her family was wonderful. Your grandfather was chairman of the Assembly of the Nobility in Saratov, Anna.'

Anna is astonished:

'Is that true? I never knew that. Mama never told me.'

'Well, pretend I never told you. There are many things it's best not to know.

'How hard it all is, how very hard . . . And I have no idea where my husband is, Anna. It's been five years already. I'm on my way to the archives now . . . to see if I can find any documents.'

Old Kossel, with his doctor's bag, in a karakul hat and tall galoshes, stands by the reception at the hotel.

'I received a call to see someone in room thirty-six. Was it you who called me?' he says sternly.

'Yes. The guest in that room is ill, he asked for a doctor. I'll show you the way.'

She stands up and leads Kossel to the room. Kossel knocks. After a brief pause, Maier's voice is heard.

'Come in!'

The receptionist goes inside, along with the doctor.

'The doctor is here to see you.'

'Thank you very much,' replies Maier, who is lying in bed.

He has covered himself with both the hotel blanket and his sheepskin coat. He shivers with the chills.

The receptionist goes out, and Kossel takes off his coat. He washes his hands, then goes over to the desk lamp to warm his frozen fingers on it.

'Well, what seems to be the problem?' the doctor asks, taking out some papers. 'Name, please . . .'

'Maier, Rudolf Ivanovich.'

'When did you arrive here, Rudolf Ivanovich?' the old man asks in a manner that expresses true interest, not just a duty to fill out an official form.

'Yesterday evening,' Maier says. He coughs.

'Well, well, let's take a look at you.' Kossel goes to wash his hands again, comes back, and sits down on a chair next to Maier.

'Hmm, I see. Yes, chills, fever. You'll have to get undressed, I'm afraid,' Kossel says apologetically.

Maier pushes the blanket off his body with difficulty. The doctor lays his palm just under the throat, then begins to tap. Then he places his ear on the chest, and on the back.

'Cough?'

'A strong cough. And it's hard to breathe. I feel like my lungs are blocked up,' Maier says. And begins to cough again.

'Yes, yes. Just as I thought,' Kossel replied. 'Laboured breathing, wheezing, especially strong on the left side. I'm guessing it's lobar pneumonia. You'll need to go to hospital. Hospitalization . . .'

'Someone's calling. Come, answer the phone! Hurry! Hurry!' Maier says suddenly, quite distinctly.

Kossel looks closely at the patient.

'What did you say?' he asks.

'The little girl is jumping, careful, she might fall down . . .'

'Oh dear, this doesn't look good, my dear fellow!' Kossel murmurs, and dials a number.

Across Petrovka, past Petrovsky Monastery, the ambulance drives towards the Petrovsky Gates, then turns in at the entrance gates of the former Ekaterininskaya Hospital. Large snowflakes fall sparsely from the sky. It's late evening. There are few passers-by. Everything seems to happen in slow motion – the snow falls slowly, the ambulance drives slowly, and the gates seem to open with reluctance.

Dr Sorin is at the reception desk. Maier is brought in on a stretcher.

'Bring the patient in here,' Sorin says to the orderlies who have transported the sick man. 'And put the papers on the desk.'

'Here. Sign, please,' says an orderly, holding out a piece of paper. Sorin signs. The orderlies leave. Sorin looks at the paper, glances over at Maier from a distance, and picks up the telephone.

'Station Two? Lena? Is Nina Ivanovna there? When she gets back, tell her to come to her station immediately.'

Sorin examines Maier. He is in a semi-conscious state.

He coughs and spits out whitish-pink sputum. Sorin raises the phlegm up to the lamp, peers at it, then feels around under the patient's armpits and groin.

He notices a cut on the neck.

He takes Maier's coat and draws the documents from the chest pocket – Party membership card, army service card, a card with the words 'Hotel Moscow, room 36' on it . . .

The last document he examines is an entry pass that reads: 'Anti-Plague Institute'.

He walks over to Maier. Maier's eyes are closed. He's coughing. Sorin looks at the paper again.

'Patient, can you hear me? What is your name?' he says, and looks at Maier, waiting for a reply.

'Yes, it's . . . Maier, Rudolf Johan . . . Ivanovich . . . Mask, the mask . . . it slipped down. By accident,' Maier mutters, and a vague, disjointed picture forms in Sorin's mind: a telephone call, a knock on the door, the voice of Galya, the porter, and Maier's reply – 'I'm coming!' And the open edge of a mask, where the sealing ring had slipped down.

'The mask, the mask . . . phone call for you . . .' Maier babbles.

'Just so. Delirium,' Sorin ascertains, and dials another number.

Sorin undresses Maier carefully, takes a hospital gown out of the cupboard, and prepares an injection of some kind.

*

Meanwhile, Tonya Sorin is standing on the stairwell landing with her friend, Nina Ivanovna, the A & E nurse. Nina Ivanovna is smoking. Tonya says:

'Well, you know, he was counting on me taking the place of his mama, hoping that I would bake cakes for him and pop them in his mouth. I don't want to!'

'Tonya, think about it, what is it that you want? When you got married, did you think your husband would be the one making soup for you?'

'Do you know the kinds of suitors I used to have?' Tonya says proudly.

'No matter who your suitors were, once you got married, you'd end up making his soup and washing his stinky socks. Even if he was the best suitor in the whole world. And let me tell you, your Alexander Matveevich is a very decent man. Believe me,' Nina Ivanovna insists.

'But I'm so bored with him, Nina, bored! We don't go to the cinema, or to the theatre, or out dancing. When he's not on duty, he just sits there reading medical books. I'm still young . . . and besides – he's a Jew . . .'

'Alexander Matveevich, open up! Why have you shut yourself up in here?' the nurse says through the door. She has just come back from her smoking break.

'Nina Ivanovna! We're in an emergency. I've locked the door, it's likely we'll have to enforce a quarantine,' Sorin responds.

'Why? What has happened? Alexander Matveevich, please forgive me for being absent.'

'Nina Ivanovna, it doesn't matter now. Maybe it's for the best. Please, take the key from the porter and lock the entrance door to accident and emergency from the outside.'

'Alexander Matveevich! Open the door!' Nina Ivanovna shouts.

She continues to pound on the door, but Sorin doesn't say another word. He pulls a blanket over Maier, who is still coughing and has now started to moan, and continues his examination.

'How did you get the cut?'

'A razor . . . at the barber's . . . a marvellous blade . . .'

Sorin goes to the telephone.

'Larisa Grigorievna, connect me right away to Lev Alexandrovich Sikorsky. It's an emergency . . . Please give me his number at home, then. Yes, it's a matter of the greatest urgency. I wouldn't disturb him otherwise. Yes, at my insistence . . .'

He notes down the number, hangs up the receiver, and dials again.

'I'd like to speak to Lev Alexandrovich, please. This is

Dr Sorin, on duty in accident and emergency. Please call him to the phone, this is an extremely urgent matter. No, I cannot make a decision without him . . . Please understand, he is the chief physician at the hospital, and there are decisions that I can't make without his consent. Yes, precisely! I insist!'

He waits by the phone.

'Lev Alexandrovich, Sorin here. I'm sorry to disturb you, but a patient has arrived here, and I have reason to suspect a case of the plague. As far as I can judge, the patent is suffering from a form of it that affects the lungs. Y. *pestis*! Of course, we must summon the infectious disease specialist. We must! Unfortunately, I have little doubt about it. The clinical picture is a classic one. And there is one more important circumstance: the patient is employed at the Anti-Plague Institute. Evidently, yes. He is isolated. A & E is in lockdown. Luckily, the nurse had just stepped out for a moment when the patient was brought in, so I'm alone here with the patient.'

Sorin speaks with precision, and suddenly acquires a self-mastery that seems rather uncharacteristic. He draws himself up, assuming an almost military bearing.

'We must take immediate measures. Quarantine – without delay. I'm afraid I have no more need for a protective suit. Lev Alexandrovich, I'm no longer a student. I'm a doctor. Good. I don't think the Commissariat of Health will be able to manage this. It's for another agency altogether . . . Thank you.'

Sorin hangs up the phone. Goes over to Maier and tries to make him more comfortable. He brings him some water to drink. He puts a compress on his forehead. Then he takes a standard form and begins to write: 'Medical History'.

Sorin stands up and leans over Maier, who opens his eyes:

'Put on mask . . . dangerous . . . Strain highly virulent . . . a mask . . . Barber, the barber . . . fact very important. Barber at the hotel . . .'

'What? What did you say?' Sorin is unsure whether the patient is delirious, or completely aware of what he is saying.

'Must be isolated. Koshkin, or Kotov . . . name starts with K . . .'

Sorin leans closer to Maier:

'I don't understand you. Are you saying something I should know?'

'Hotel barber . . . close contact . . . quarantine urgent . . .'

Sorin nods.

'Yes, yes, of course. And the barber . . . I'll get word to him, don't worry, Rudolf Ivanovich.'

Maier tosses and turns, he gasps for air. There is pink

foam on his lips. Sweat drips from his forehead. Sorin wipes his face . . .

He makes another call:

'Lev Alexandrovich? I'm sorry to disturb you again, this is Sorin. The patient informs me that he came into close contact the evening before with the barber from the Hotel Moscow. He must be isolated at once, it's the highest priority. The patient can't recall the name – Koshkin or Kotov. Something starting with K . . . Thank you. If we don't take drastic measures, there's risk of an epidemic. He is the first one we must isolate. Right away. He can be brought here to us for the time being. Temporarily. But all others who have come into contact with the patient should be taken to Sokolinaya Gora, the main hospital for infectious diseases. They are specially equipped for it . . .'

Lev Alexandrovich Sikorsky is on the phone. He is talking to the NKVD Commissar of Public Health.

'Sikorsky speaking, chief physician of Ekaterininskaya Hospital. Yakov Stepanovich, a matter of the utmost urgency prompts me to call you at this hour. We have a case of the plague in my hospital. Pneumonic plague. No, I can't come to see you. I'm already at the hospital. Yes, of course.'

The Commissar speaks, and Sikorsky responds:

'I am, in fact, already in quarantine. All measures have been taken in the hospital. I will be here until the quarantine is lifted, so I ask that you take all the necessary measures to track down those who have been exposed to our patient and to isolate them without delay. I think it would be highly expedient to involve the security forces in the matter. Who is more capable of tracking down those who have possibly been infected than they? Yakov Stepanovich, we have two people isolated here in accident and emergency: Maier, the patient himself, and his attending doctor, Sorin. They are the primary risk group. There is still another possible carrier of the infection, and I request that you isolate him at once, and transport him, with extreme caution, to A & E – this is the barber at the Hotel Moscow, someone by the name of Koshkin or Kotov. Highest risk group. We'll be in touch. I'll be waiting for your call.'

The Commissar of Public Health sits next to the phone, bewildered. Dials a number. Puts down the receiver. Dials again.

A phone call marathon is under way. People pick up receivers, dial, put them down again. We see a multitude of faces, military men, plain-clothes officers, bosses, and subordinates . . .

*

Hospital corridor. Two figures in masks push the barber through the door into accident and emergency. They lock the door behind him.

'Do you have any idea what this is all about?' one of the masked men asks the other.

'You're a very curious fellow, Comrade Lieutenant. It's none of our business,' the second one says.

'Well, it's just that we don't usually work this way. And why a hospital?'

'The less you know, the better you sleep . . .'

Sorin stands up and goes to meet Veniamin Alexeevich Kotikov, the barber who was just thrust into the receiving room. The barber is in a state of panic.

'What is going on? Today is my day off, and suddenly they come to get me, they take me away, without telling me anything . . . I didn't know what to think, I started imagining goodness knows what . . .'

Sorin is prepared for this discussion.

'Please calm down. I'm a doctor. My name is Sorin. Listen to me, Veniamin Alexeevich. You and I are both in quarantine. We have been exposed to a patient with the plague. Both of us. Yesterday evening you shaved a man who was brought to the hospital. He was given a preliminary diagnosis of the plague,' Sorin says without emotion.

'What are you saying?' the barber blurts out. 'What do you mean, the plague? And what right do you have to bring me here?'

'It's pneumonic plague. A highly infectious disease.'

The barber takes off his cap and covers his mouth and nose with it.

'That's right. The less you talk, the better. Now listen carefully. We are both in quarantine. I am too. This entire floor is sealed off. Now I will take you to a room adjacent to this one and lock you inside. Food will be brought to you. I won't come in, at least until such time as you need me and I am in a position to help. Get up now, and let's go.'

The barber stands up with difficulty. His legs won't obey him, and he clutches the doctor's arm. He looks faint and miserable. Alexander Matveevich feels stronger and more confident with every passing minute.

Sorin leads the barber to the next room. This is the nurses' room.

'You should try to make yourself comfortable here for the time being,' Sorin says. 'Please be patient, we'll fix it up . . .'

The barber moves his cap away from his face and bursts into tears.

'My God! My God! But I have to call home! I have a wife, a daughter!' the barber says, between sobs.

'They will be notified. I advise you not to try leaving this room,' Sorin says, and goes out, locking the door behind him. He crosses the corridor, goes up to the door on to the stairwell, and pushes it – locked. The first priority – making sure he is cut off from the rest of the hospital – has been accomplished.

Sikorsky dials a number. The guard in the entrance lodge picks up.

'Who? Who's speaking? Ah, Lev Alexandrovich! I didn't recognize you at first.'

'Good evening, Petrovich. Good evening. This is an order. Lock the gates tightly, switch your telephone line straight to my number, and don't let anyone in. No one. Is that clear? Not a single creature, not even a bird.'

'But how can I? Ambulances drive up, loaded with sick folk – what, I have to turn them away too?' the old man says, perplexed.

'I'm telling you – no one. Only with my express permission. And don't leave your post for a second. Is that clear?' Sikorsky says again.

'Clear as can be. How could it not be? We've been working together for twenty years!' the porter says, nodding his head, then asks again: 'Not even the ambulances?'

'Upon my word . . . I'm telling you: no one at all! I'll send assistance to you,' Sikorsky says, and hangs up.

The porter stays put, and grumbles:

'He'll send assistance. Assistance, hell. As though I couldn't manage on my own . . .'

Sikorsky's office. He's wearing a mask. He has summoned all the doctors on duty from their wards. There are around ten of them. They are all alarmed. They whisper.

'Maybe . . . it's the Big Boss himself?' one doctor asks another, in a low tone charged with meaning. The other shrugs, and responds.

'Seems Sikorsky called everyone together. Is it an inspection?'

'Doesn't look like it. No. Must be something else.'

Sikorsky rises when the last of the doctors on duty has arrived and stands next to his armchair. No one speaks.

'Colleagues,' he begins solemnly. 'Today we will all undergo a coming-of-age test at our hospital, an endurance test of our civic and professional mettle. We have the plague on our hands.'

The silence is deafening. Sikorsky speaks again.

'Pneumonic plague – in accident and emergency. One of our comrades has already locked himself in with the patient; thus, the first stage of the quarantine procedures has been carried out. We must now do everything within our capacity to guard against an epidemic. We have the

43

resources. We will be assisted in our efforts, but there are a number of organizational measures that we must adopt and execute ourselves. Are there infectious disease doctors among us?'

Within the immobile crowd, a small woman stirs, and says: 'I've worked with infectious diseases. I worked on cholera, in Central Asia.'

'Very good. I appoint you my deputy for the quarantine. We must consider ourselves to be at war. Now then, my first orders: we immediately seal the exits to the stairwells and cut off all passage between floors. You will depart to execute this order exactly one minute after we have all decided one other extremely important matter. At present there are about two hundred patients. In order to avoid panic, we must come up with a version of the situation that will not cause too much alarm and stress. We must announce that we have declared a quarantine because of . . .'

'Infectious jaundice?' someone suggests hesitantly.

'No, that won't work. Botkin's disease, as a rule, doesn't recur after the first bout, and we'd have to discharge all those who have already had it. It must be a kind of illness that doesn't result in immunity.'

'Recurring typhoid fever!' someone says, and the doctors become a bit more animated.

'Too severe.'

44

'Influenza!' says the small woman who knows about infectious diseases.

'Perfect!' Sikorsky exclaims. 'It's a dangerous disease, but with a relatively low mortality rate. And the word is pleasant, but not completely comprehensible. That's decided, then: quarantine due to an outbreak of influenza. This is the explanation we will give the patients. I would ask that you gather the mid-level medical personnel together and inform them about what is happening, making them aware of the seriousness of the situation. Now I ask you to go back to your departments, and I hope we will come through this . . . skirmish . . . honourably.' Sikorsky suddenly smiles. 'All orders will be transmitted by phone. I wish you luck.'

Sorin goes up to Maier and tries to make him more comfortable. He gives him some water, then puts the compress on his head again. Maier's breathing is ragged. Sorin leaves the room and moves over to the next door:

'Have you settled in, Veniamin Alexeevich? Do you need anything?'

'Yes, I certainly do need something! How can this have happened? They snatched me in broad daylight! What right do you have? It's cold in here! Bring me a blanket!'

'Right away,' Sorin says without opening the door.

He returns to his own office, takes another standard form, and again begins to write: 'Medical History'.

The NKVD Commissar of Health has an audience with a Very High Personage, second only to the Big Boss, who speaks with a Georgian accent.* The Very High Personage is indignant.

'It's beyond me, Yakov Stepanovich. What is the nature of our responsibility? If it's a matter of wrecking or sabotage, rest assured the guilty will be punished! Swiftly punished! In that case, you wouldn't even have to ask. We'll find them! We'll punish them!'

'I don't think this is a matter of sabotage, but of criminal negligence by a scientific researcher trying to create an anti-plague vaccine,' the Commissar of Health says carefully.

'And criminal negligence is a punishable offence! We will punish!' the Very High Personage says, reaffirming his original thesis. The Commissar of Health makes one more attempt to shift the course of the discussion.

---

* Editor's note: Lavrentiy Beria (1899–1953), the exceptionally brutal chief of the NKVD. Beria was of Mingrelian heritage, and grew up in Georgia. After Stalin's death, he was eventually found guilty of treason, terrorism and counter-revolutionary activity, and was tried and executed on 23 December 1953.

'If all those who have come into contact with the patient in the past two days are not isolated within forty-eight hours, an epidemic of the plague is possible.'

'Do we have lists?'

'We are drawing them up. If there is any delay, the possible extent of the disaster is unfathomable. During the last global epidemic, a third of the population of Europe died.'

'A third?' the High Personage says, astonished.

'Yes. A third.'

'When did that happen?' the Personage asks, his interest piqued.

'In the fourteenth century. Thirteen forty, or thereabouts.'

'Tch!' The Personage sucks his teeth. 'How large was the population back then? Very small.'

'In a modern city, with our density of population, the epidemic could spread like wildfire and infect the entire populace. Do you understand?' the Commissar says wearily.

'Very well.' The High Personage stands up abruptly. 'We'll help. We'll help with the lists, and with the liquidation.'

The Commissar of Health freezes.

'No, no, we're only talking about quarantine. Not liquidation. It is necessary that we collect and isolate all those who have been exposed to the patient as soon as possible.

The quicker we do this, the greater our chances of warding off the epidemic.'

The Very High Personage looks down at the Commissar of Health haughtily, with a hint of mockery:

'We can assist in that too. The means at our disposal are legion . . .'

The Commissar of Health is being driven through the night-time city, sitting next to his chauffeur. The apartment blocks are all dark; only in the larger buildings of official organizations are the lights still burning. Occasional street lamps. Snow.

The Very High Personage washes his hands in the bathroom, looks in the mirror at his reflection. He takes a gulp of water, swirls it around in his mouth, and spits into the sink.

The traffic is blocked along Petrovka Street and Strastnoy Boulevard. Warning signs and posts erected. Columns of military vehicles enter the city. The district of Sokolinaya Gora has been cordoned off.

The Commissar of Health is conducting a meeting. A telephone receiver is on the table next to him. Sikorsky is on the

48

line. Among those present are several Health Commissariat officials who are also doctors, academicians, representatives of National Security, and a High Personage.

The chief physician of infectious diseases reports:

'The three inner quarantine rings in the hospital – the wards, the floors, and the hospital building itself – have been secured by orderlies. But the supervision and enforcement of the two outer belts – on the hospital grounds and outside, in the environs – is beyond our capacity.'

'Write that down,' the High Personage says to his assistant, nodding.

The chief physician of infectious diseases continues:

'There are three contact groups. The patient had contact on the train, at the board meeting, and in the hotel. The most dangerous cohort is the group in the hotel, since that contact took place at the stage of the illness when the patient was most contagious. They were the people he had contact with just before his hospitalization. Here I will point out that for the next twenty-four hours, the infected still do not pose any danger to others who are exposed to them. For that reason, full isolation of all contacts can guarantee our success. On the other hand, if one of the passengers on the train was infected, that person could be a source of contagion.'

*

A sheet of paper with the words '1. Hospital: Kotikov, Ozerova, Sozonova, Anadurdyeva'. The first name is already crossed out. 'Anadurdyeva' has a tick beside it.

That page is laid aside. Underneath it is another page that reads: '2. List of members of the board of the Commissariat of Health'. The hand puts a tick next to the names.

Numerous garage doors fling open simultaneously all over town. Black Marias* exit, driving through the night-time city.

The deep hours of the night. The wind is still. The snow that was coming down all evening now blankets the streets and pavements. In the nocturnal silence you can distinctly hear approaching vehicles. Two of them drive up to a building. Eight soldiers wearing sheepskin coats jump out of one, and from the other emerge two people wearing protective suits. The soldiers cordon off the courtyard, then form a corridor along which the two in protective suits pass through the entrance. They disappear inside.

Grigoriev, chairman of the board of the Commissariat of Public Health, is asleep in his apartment. The doorbell

---

* Cf. editor's note on p. 117. 'Black Maria' was the nickname for the feared NKVD vehicle.

rings. His wife lifts her head, covered in curling papers, from the pillow.

'Volya, someone's at the door! Volya!' her eyes express terror.

'Um-m,' Grigoriev moans in his sleep. 'Um-m-m.'

'Volya! Someone's ringing the bell!' His wife sits up in bed. 'Should I open it?'

'What?' Grigoriev wakes up. 'Who's ringing?'

'I don't know. Should I open it?' his wife says, already pulling a robe around her.

'Ask who it is,' Grigoriev says, fully awake now. 'No, never mind. I'll go myself,' Grigoriev says, stopping her. He goes into the hall, yanks open the door, and recoils, on seeing two figures in protective suits. A muffled voice says:

'Comrade Grigoriev?'

'Yes, I'm Grigoriev.'

'Please get dressed at once and follow us.'

'What's the matter? Has something happened?' Grigoriev asks.

'Everything will be explained to you when we get there. You may tell your family that you have been called away on an urgent business trip.'

His wife pokes her head into the hallway, and when she sees the two figures in protective gear, utters a piercing scream.

'Hurry up. Get ready, and don't bring anything with you. We're waiting by the door,' the mysterious, muffled voice in a mask says, and closes the door behind him.

The two figures in protective suits stand outside the door, one on the right, one on the left. The door opens, and Grigoriev emerges, wearing a fur hat and coat. One of the masked figures tries to pull a mask over Grigoriev's face. Grigoriev jumps aside in alarm.

'No, don't worry, Vsevolod Alexandrovich. You'll have all the explanation you need in a few minutes,' the man says reassuringly, and, taking his hand gently, leads him down the staircase.

Next to the entrance, a Black Maria is waiting, and Grigoriev is placed inside. The vehicle drives off. In the first-floor window, an old woman's face framed in two limp, greasy pigtails, appears. The old woman leans out of the window, her eyes wide with astonishment.

A jumble of doorbells by the door of a communal apartment, and a name next to each bell: Redkin, Tsintsiper, Zhurkin, Rodionov, Speransky.

A figure in a sheepskin coat runs his fingers over the buttons and presses when he locates the one he wants: Zhurkin.

He rings – no sound. He rings three more times. Listens. Two figures in protective suits come up the stairs.

'Did you ring? No sound? Maybe the bell is broken,' one of them says.

'Ring again! The bell rings in the room, you can't hear it from here,' says the other.

Finally, they hear footsteps, and the jangling of the latch.

The outline of Ida Zhurkin's tousled head appears in the doorway. The figure in the sheepskin coat thrusts some kind of illegible document under her nose. Ida backs away.

'I need to see Comrade Zhurkin right away,' says Sheepskin, very politely, lodging his foot by the doorjamb on the threshold.

'What exactly is the matter?'

'Are you Alexei Ivanovich's wife?' he says.

'Yes, I'm his spouse,' Ida says with an air of dignity.

'Then get going,' he says, almost gruffly. Ida hurries down the corridor to their room, with Sheepskin right behind her. The two figures in protective suits bring up the rear. Alexei Ivanovich is standing by the bed, pulling on his trousers.

'What's going on out there?' he asks his wife in alarm.

'They've come for you!' Ida says, horror-struck.

'Who?' The question answers itself.

Ida sees the figure enter, and she sinks down on a stool.

'Get ready to go at once, Alexei Ivanovich,' says Sheepskin.

Ida takes a deep breath and tries to collect her thoughts.

'Alexei, listen to me carefully. There must be some sort of mistake. I'm certain this will be cleared up, and they'll let you go free.'

The two in the protective suits enter the room.

'Ida, pack my things,' Alexei Ivanovich says to her.

'Alexei, what things? They'll let you go!' Ida cries.

'Warm things. Wool socks, my grey sweater, long underwear . . .' Alexei enumerates. Ida, meanwhile, is already collecting his socks. As fate would have it, they all have holes.

'Don't bring anything,' Sheepskin says.

'But what is the problem?' Zhurkin asks, belatedly.

'Excuse us for the interruption,' Sheepskin says gently, rolling the document between his hands. 'We won't keep you for long. Your presence is mandatory. I'm not authorized to say why. They will explain it all when we get there.'

'You see, Alexei? What did I tell you!' Ida clings to her husband's woollen overcoat; he strokes her soft head, and leaves.

The door slams behind him. On the landing, two strong hands grasp him, pulling a protective mask over his face.

'Agh!' Alexei feels he might choke.

'Easy! Easy, Comrade Zhurkin! Get into the car, please.'
The car roars off.

Dr Kossel is lying on a pile of fluffed-up pillows. His expression is careworn and tired.

'Dina! Dina! Come to bed!'

In an armchair, staring at a portrait of a young man in an airman's uniform, sits an older woman with a distracted, vacant expression on her still-beautiful face. She wears a nightgown, she is clutching her hairpins in her hand, and her sparse grey hair hangs down on her shoulders.

'Dina! Come to bed, my dear!' Kossel urges again.

The old woman shakes her head – not in response to her husband, but as though at her own thoughts.

'No, no, no,' she whispers.

Old Kossel puts his feet down on the floor.

Three men walk down the long corridor of the elegant Nirnsee Building where the Kossels live. One wears a sheepskin coat and the other two are in protective suits. They ring the bell of the apartment.

'A rather late hour for visiting,' Kossel mutters.

The bell doesn't alarm the old man in the least. He is used to being disturbed at all hours. He pulls on his robe and shuffles out to answer the door. His wife doesn't budge from her place.

'How may I help you, dear fellow?' he asks the one in the sheepskin coat.

The young man holds out a document, but Kossel pushes his hand aside.

'How may I help you?' he asks again.

'You are summoned to appear without delay,' the young man replies.

'Excuse me, who has fallen ill?' the old man says.

The young man rolls up the document between his hands again.

'Come inside, come inside, I'll just get my glasses. I can't see a thing without them.'

Kossel grabs his glasses, and peers, finally, at the document.

'Yes, yes, I see. And how may I help you?' the old man says.

'You are summoned to appear without delay,' repeats the young man, who is already getting fed up with the uncomprehending old man.

'Well, without delay it is, then. You will have to wait, however, until I get ready. Old people grow so slow and feeble, you know . . .' Kossel grasps his wife firmly by the shoulder. 'Dina, go and lie down.'

Dina gets up from her chair obediently and walks over to the bed.

Kossel gets dressed. The young man stares a while at the portrait in its black frame of mourning.

'Your son?' the young man says. 'An Arctic pilot? That same Kossel they wrote about in the papers?'

'The same.'

Kossel puts on his round fur hat and his fur coat with a shawl collar; he begins to look like a provincial priest. His wife turns to him and says, surprisingly clearly:

'Come back soon. I don't like being alone.'

'I'll be back soon, soon . . .' He swallows the words that he was about to say, kisses the old woman's dry head, and leaves.

'Shall I turn out the light?' he asks by the door.

'Don't! Leave it on!' his wife says.

The Petrovskys. An ordinary family in an ordinary apartment. Night. A woman, no longer young, paces the room, rocking a crying child in her arms. She stops by the window and sees a Black Maria drive up and park by the entrance of their building.

'Fedya! Fedya!' the woman shouts. 'Look! They've come for us!'

Fedya, a middle-aged man, goes up to the window.

'They've already been here. Isn't there anyone else they want to take?'

'They haven't taken everyone else's daughter already! Don't you understand?'

Fedya looks out the window. Four figures are getting out of the car, and three of them walk up to the entrance. The child wails.

'Leave quickly, Fedya.'

'What do you mean?'

'Use the backstairs. Hurry! You're as stubborn as a child . . .'

The child screams.

Fedya puts on his coat and grabs his fur hat with the long laces on the ear flaps.

The doorbell sounds.

'Run to Leningrad Station and go to Bologoe, to Aunt Klava's. And sit tight. Well, don't just stand there! Get a move on!'

She stuffs some money into his hand.

He goes down the corridor, opens the latch to the back door, and leaves by the backstairs.

The doorbell rings.

The little wheels of apparatuses spin and whir, telegraph and telephone lines crackle, sheets of paper lie on heavy, official tables, and piles of folders grow higher and higher.

Someone's hand circles the names on the long list of members of the board of the Commissariat of Public Health. It ticks them off. Only one name has not been circled: 'Esinsky'.

The corridor of Hotel Moscow. Two men in masks haul in a barrel of disinfectant. Two others spray the rooms. A thorough disinfection is under way. Two more examine the book with the names of hotel guests and the rooms they occupy. The same circles and ticks. Two names are circled with thick red pencil: Anadurdyeva, and Kotikov. One of the men asks another:

'What do we do with this one? She checked out.'

'Ah, the People's Deputy of the Supreme Soviet. Averin, call over there to the accountant. They'll have a record of the ticket she got. We'll take her off the train.'

'And Kotikov?'

'The barber? He had a day off today, they sent a car in the morning to take him from home . . .'

'To Sokolinaya?'

'No, they weren't ready there. They took him to Sorin, to Ekaterininskaya Hospital. There are three of them there now – Maier, Sorin, and that barber. They're locked in A & E.'

*

The windows of the houses are all dark. Colonel Pavlyuk is lying on his divan, in the darkness of his study. Downstairs, by the entrance, he hears car doors slam. He gets up and goes over to the window. He listens. The lift door slams shut. The doorbell rings. Pavlyuk exits his study and goes to his wife's room.

'What is it?' she asks.

'Go to the door. But don't open it before three minutes have passed.'

'For you?' In a flash, wide awake, she raises her eyes to her husband.

'You understand?' Pavlyuk says.

'Yes.'

'Go.'

'Sergei! Sergei!'

'None of that, now. Quiet, please.' And he goes back to his study.

His wife hurries to the door. The bell sounds relentlessly, without ceasing. Pavlyuk opens the bottom drawer of his desk. From its depths, he takes out an envelope, and places it in the centre of his tidy, bare desk. On the envelope is written: 'To Comrade Stalin'.

Natalya, Pavlyuk's wife, stands at the door. Her hand rests on the door handle. She opens it slowly. There, in the door frame, is the smiling pink face of a man in a sheepskin coat.

'My, you're a sound sleeper!' he says, still smiling. 'Is Comrade Pavlyuk at home?'

From the study, the sound of a shot rings out.

Christmas tree. New Year's Eve revelry in a low-ceilinged, semi-rural interior. Sweaty, ample women; bare, thick hands; creased necks. Gramophone music, husky and heart-rending. On a plate in the middle of the table is a roasted goose, only partially consumed, its outline clearly defined around a mass of stewed cabbage. One man, having yanked down part of the lace doily from the shelf above, is now sleeping on the kitchen sofa. Another brandishes a piece of the goose, then stuffs it in the face of someone who's tipsy, but still hasn't fallen under the table. This is the goose breeder who was travelling in Maier's train compartment.

'Come on, just try it, try it, Semyon! Klava baked them with cabbage, with cabbage, God damn it, and Verka with apples! With apples! Just try it, Semyon!'

But Semyon waves him off.

'Kolya, can't you understand? They lived with me for three years, they were like little children to me, and I was their mother, I can't eat them!'

'No, Semyon, you're wrong! Just try it, I tell you. My Klava bakes them with cabbage . . . I'm begging you!' And

Kolya keeps pushing a piece of the goose up into Semyon's face.

'Go to hell!' Semyon says.

'Leave him be!'

'Leave him alone!' says the woman with the bare, thick hands and ample breasts.

'Sit down,' Kolya shouts at her.

But the woman bends over and snatches the piece of goose from his hand with her teeth. Everyone starts laughing, except Semyon, who suddenly puts his head in his hands and bursts into tears. The other woman, younger, but also sturdily built, sits down next to him and tries to comfort him.

'Semyon, listen, Semyon, don't be sad, you'll just breed some new ones!'

Semyon weeps, mopping his eyes, and his girlfriend leans against his side.

'I just don't understand it! And it wasn't even that cold, they survived when it was much colder, at home. Why did they have to die?'

'Don't get all upset about it, Semyon, you can breed new ones, you'll see!' his girlfriend insists.

'Of course I'll breed them! Even if it takes ten years, however many I have to destroy, I'll succeed with at least one.'

'Of course you will, Semyon, of course you will!' the girlfriend says.

On the porch, two figures are standing, and a third runs up to them from the house next door, waving his hand.

'Let's go, this one here is number eighteen!'

They knock on the porch door, pull the handle – the door opens wide, and all three figures bundle into the mud-room of the house, clouds of steam billowing around them. A torch flips on, casting a circle of light on the inner door, and they start knocking vigorously.

'Open up, Klava, Belash is here!' Kolya commands.

'It's the middle of the night, why would Belash come round?' she says, but opens the door. Kolya gives a low whistle, and Klava, arms akimbo, says insolently:

'Well, well, well. What have we here? Gatecrashers!'

The uninvited guests are momentarily confused, but not for long. Their leader quickly recovers his composure and asks:

'Is Citizen Kulkov here?'

'Yes, he is,' the girlfriend says saucily. 'Right here, in fact.'

'I'd like a minute with you,' the leader says.

Semyon stands up uncertainly.

'I'm Kulkov.'

'Come outside, this matter concerns you alone.'

63

Everyone stands up at once and falls silent. Only the gramophone keeps up its wheezing.

Four figures walk down the path from the house – in front walks Semyon, and the other three trail behind him.

Sorin inserts the needle into Maier's upper arm. Maier is lying on the examining table in accident and emergency. He's undressed. His face is distorted, he's gripped by an attack of coughing. Bloody foam appears on his lips.

Sorin sits down and writes: '2.30 a.m. Temperature . . . pulse. Conditions . . .'

Kotikov the barber is lying on a makeshift bed, several chairs pushed together, in the nurses' room next door. He gets up, goes to the door, knocks and shouts:

'Doctor! Doctor!'

Sorin goes over to the door.

'What's the matter, Veniamin Alexeevich?' Sorin says.

'I need to get out! I have to use the toilet.'

'I'll bring you a bucket, Veniamin Alexeevich. Wait a moment,' Sorin says wearily.

'No, no, I don't want a bucket! I need to get out of here! You understand?' the barber says with desperation in his voice.

'Out of the question, Veniamin Alexeevich! You may not

come out under any circumstances! Wait a moment, please.'
Sorin goes to fetch a bucket. He takes it to the door . . .

An operations room at Kazan Station in Moscow. Fevered activity. One person is leafing through some pages, scribbled over with crosses and ticks and circles.

'This train was fitted out in Saratov, and the train crew was from Astrakhan. Right?'

'No, you'll have to find out from the crew chief. He's the only one who could know that information.'

'Call him at the railway workers' hostel.'

Someone immediately gets on the phone.

'Is the name Kozelkov?'

'The crew chief? Yes. Kozelkov, Ivan Lukyanovich.'

A group of people in the station restaurant. Military men: three dashing lieutenants. Their companions – two young women, one of whom is the conductor from the train Maier travelled on. The conductor says flirtatiously:

'But I really do like my job. It's impossible for me to stay in one place. And you meet all kinds of people, sometimes even very interesting ones.'

'We don't like staying in one place, either, that's for sure. Right, Volodya?'

*

The search for the conductor continues in the operations room.

'Rodionov, you go and pick up Kozelkov. We'll sort things out when he gets here.'

A woman sobs and clings to the man in the sheepskin coat:

'I can't! I can't! Let me go! My baby is too little! I'm still breastfeeding! The child will die!'

The man carefully peels off the woman, trying to persuade her:

'There's no point in making such a fuss, it's an official matter!'

Another figure calls him aside, and whispers something to him.

'Well, all right, you may bring your child.'

The woman hastily gets her child ready, wraps it in a warm blanket, takes a supply of nappies, and moans:

'My God, what is this about, what is this about . . .'

Kotikov the barber kicks the door with his feet. He shouts:

'Let me out! What are you keeping me in here for? I'm healthy, I'm perfectly healthy!'

He coughs. Gasps for breath. Then shouts again:

'I'll lodge a complaint! I have connections! They'll punish you! Open up!'

Sorin is sitting next to Maier in the examining room. He takes Maier's hand in his, and measures his pulse. Maier is failing.

'Letter . . . letter . . .' Maier whispers.

Sorin leans over him with a glass of water:

'Take a sip.'

Maier shakes his head . . .

Sorin hears the commotion in the next room and hurries to the door:

'One moment, I'll be with you shortly.'

He returns to his office, takes a syringe, fills it with liquid, puts on a mask, and walks back down the corridor to the barber, who continues bashing on the door. Sorin unlocks the door, opens it, and slips inside the room:

'Calm down, please. I'll give you a little injection. Please don't worry. Sleep a bit. How are you feeling now?'

'I was feeling wonderful. Yesterday, and today too! But now I'm feeling unwell. On what grounds are you . . .'

'Yes, yes, very good. Let's take your temperature . . .'

He puts the thermometer in his mouth. Gives him an injection.

'You've got all wound up. Now you'll be able to relax. The main thing is not to get too agitated. True, it's unpleasant. Someone was infected with a contagious disease, you came into contact with him, and now you have to be quarantined. Everyone who came into contact with him has to be hospitalized and quarantined . . . You do have a high temperature . . . I'm going to bring you a pillow and blanket now. Just lie down.'

The barber begins to weep.

'Why do I have such bad luck? I've been dogged by bad luck all my life.'

Saratov. The Anti-Plague research centre. Maier's laboratory, a small, snow-covered building, is surrounded by guards. Two soldiers stand guard in the anteroom, where the porter, Galya, usually keeps watch.

Inside the restaurant of Kazan railway station in Moscow. By the door stand the two military officers from the operations room and crew chief Kozelkov, who glances around the room, then breaks into a grin.

'There she is, there's Zinka! I rode with her for two years, I know where to find her at this hour! She's over there, sitting with the military men, and Katka Enakieva is with her. Two whores, everyone knows them!'

The lieutenant from the operations room approaches Zinka, and, offering his excuses, he leads her away from the table. She goes with him, looking rather satisfied and proud.

At the restaurant entrance, she realizes that she is not being invited to dance and starts feeling rather nervous. But one of the young men takes her by the arm and ushers her out the door.

'Hey, let me go, where are you dragging me off to?' Zinka the conductor says loudly; but the young man leans over and whispers something gently in her ear.

Zinka submits to his request and follows him. They pick their way among passengers sprawled out on the floor of the station. The passengers, some of them asleep, are surrounded by parcels, muddy footwear, and howling children. She trips over a suitcase, and barks at a young woman:

'Hey, what do you think you're doing, lazing around here? Get your stuff out of the way, will you?'

The woman pulls the suitcase towards her. This woman is Anna – Maier's girlfriend. She has just arrived in Moscow and is looking for a number she needs in her notebook.

Telephones quiver and shake and ring. Numbers, names, codes. A voice announces: 'Train number twenty-seven is running two hours thirty minutes late.'

'Call Salakhov immediately. Major Siverkin. Major Siverkin.'

'Anadurdyeva, carriage number two.'

'Golosovker, Grinev, Dymchenko, Dennik, Eskina,

Erofeeva, Erofeev, Zhabotinsky, Ivanov Vladimir, Ivanov Viktor, Ignatienko, Ivina, Ilyin, Ikonnikova, Irusadze, Karpov . . .'

'List number two, list number two . . . 823/4.'

Leningrad Station in Moscow. Fedya Petrovsky buys a ticket.

A voice from the tannoy announces: 'The train to Leningrad will be leaving from track six . . .'

Petrovsky rushes out onto the platform – track one. He jumps down onto the rails and runs in the direction of track six, desperate not to miss the train. He is wearing the hat with ear flaps, its long laces dangling free. He doesn't see the oncoming train, and runs in front of it. Screeching brakes.

A hat flies out from under the train, landing in the snow. Petrovsky's body is lying on the rails . . .

Morning in Moscow. Shops are open. Housewives are hurrying past with cans: one for oil, another for paraffin. Sverbeev exits a shoe shop. He carries a big shoebox with the inscription 'Strideswift'. He stops at the first convenient spot and, leaning back against the wall, removes one worn-out old woman's boot, rather large, and puts on a brand-new man's boot that he has taken out of the box.

Two figures approach him. He stands awkwardly on one foot, leaning against the wall.

'Citizen Sverbeev?' one of them says.

'What of it?' he replies.

'Follow us,' the other says.

After stuffing his second foot into the new boot, Sverbeev falls in step, tripping over the untied laces, behind the two people in sheepskin coats.

The car roars off. In the spot where he was standing, he leaves behind a pair of worn-out boots, and a new box with the inscription 'Strideswift'.

The old woman from the train, former owner of the worn-out boots, is at her own home, on the outskirts of Tambov. An even more ancient old woman, her mother, is lying on her back in bed. Her face is dark, and her sharp nose points towards the ceiling; she almost resembles a corpse. The daughter is talking to her mother.

'Mama, you were coughing during the night, but as soon as I gave you some honey, you stopped coughing . . .'

The ancient woman, completely impassive, doesn't reply. The daughter, in turn, isn't fazed by her indifference.

'And what they used to say was to take black wormwood and dry it and boil it up. But I'm thinking – why drink that bitter stuff, wormwood, when you have honey? Savvushka brought some in August. He keeps bees, he's got about twenty hives, and he brought it over. Goddaughter, he says, take this for yourself and Grandma. See? Now it's just come in handy . . . Mama, are you asleep, or what?'

Someone knocks at the door. The woman opens up and sees two young fellows standing there, strapping lads, well fed. She is taken aback.

'Well, Elena Dmitrievna, you made it home all right?' one of them says.

The woman grows numb with fright, her legs nearly buckle under her. She sits down on a stool.

'Get ready, Granny, you're coming with us,' the older fellow says.

The woman is silent for a bit longer, and then, without warning, suddenly begins to wail:

'Sweethearts, dear ones, where are you taking me? Have pity on me, an old woman! Of what use am I to you?'

'Calm down, calm down, Elena Dmitrievna. Don't get all bent out of shape. We'll have a little talk with you, sort everything out, and then we'll deliver you back home – over the river and through the woods,' says the younger fellow acerbically.

'Deliver me, deliver me, you say, you tyrants! You'll deliver me, all right! Listen lads, I'll give them to you, just don't take me. My poor old mother over there is sick, she can't get out of bed, how can I leave her here alone, eh?'

And she darts nimbly into the mudroom. After a moment, she emerges with a wonderful pair of tall boots, lined with fur.

'I don't need someone's else's,' the old woman mutters. 'I saw them lying there, I snatched them up – but I don't need what's not mine.'

The young fellows exchange glances. One of them circles his index finger next to his temple, indicating that the old hag is off her rocker. But that doesn't change the situation.

'Come on, Granny, let's go. We're taking you for a ride in the car. Put your coat on!'

The woman flings the tall boots on the floor and starts to wail once more.

The ancient woman in the bed, not opening her eyes, blesses her daughter, saying, 'Aw, pity the bitch!'

Ludmila Ignatievna, another of Maier's companions from the train compartment, is with a new lover. Pillows are tossed around, the mattress springs heave the energetic pair up and down. A bare knee pokes out from under the blanket, then disappears, and appears again. The doorbell rings.

The mattress springs go quiet at once. The lover asks, alarmed:

'Your husband?'

'Impossible. He's away on a business trip. To the Belomorkanal . . .' Ludmila Ignatievna says. 'I won't open it.'

The doorbell keeps ringing.

'Hell's bells! Get dressed,' Ludmila Ignatievna orders.

But her lover is already up and dressed. She pulls on her stockings. The doorbell is ringing. Her skirt. Still ringing. A jacket. Ringing. She pats her hair into place.

'And me? What about me?' her new-found friend asks.

'Stay right here. Don't move.' And she hides him behind the curtain that covers the armoire.

She goes to answer the door.

'Who is it?'

'Ludmila Ignatievna Kostrikina? Open up!' says the voice in the corridor.

Her lover, sweating, squirms behind the curtain.

'Why did it take you so long to come to the door? Your neighbours told us you were at home. Put your coat on, Ludmila Ignatievna. We don't plan to detain you for long, we simply need to talk to you, to ask you a few questions, please.'

'But of course, with pleasure!' Ludmila Ignatievna smiles, puts on her fur coat, and, pulling back the curtain and making a surreptitious sign to her lover, goes out, leaving her key on the table.

*

Esinsky, the member of the board of the Commissariat of Public Health, disembarks from the train at Moscow Station in Leningrad. Two figures approach him and lead him away. He looks around helplessly, swivelling his head in all directions.

A provincial station. Train manoeuvres. One of the passenger carriages is uncoupled and shunted into a dead-end siding. Soldiers stand on the steps on either side of the carriage. The train stops. The two soldiers enter the train carriage, and the older one summons the conductor – a country fellow, tipsy, with slightly Asian features. In the conductor's cab, the soldier shows him some official documents and asks for his help.

'The carriage has been uncoupled, and will be temporarily detained. There's a Turkmen woman, one Anadurdyeva, a People's Deputy. She must be taken off the train – but quietly, without causing panic,' the lieutenant explains.

'They've already taken her,' the conductor mumbles.

'What do you mean, they've taken her?' the lieutenant says.

'They took her in Razdolsk,' the conductor says. 'Two stations back.'

'Who? Who took her?' the lieutenant shouts.

'I helped them. The ambulance came to the train, and we put her in. She was sick,' the conductor says.

'Sick with what?' The lieutenant seems to hesitate a bit before asking.

The conductor loses his temper.

'With what? With what? Her stomach, that's what! She felt sick with her stomach, so I took her off. If she'd upped and died here, I'd have been responsible for it. I've been through that once already.'

'When did you pass through Razdolsk?'

'We're running late, around five hours. We passed through Razdolsk in the night, round about two thirty,' the conductor says.

'Here's the deal. I'm posting a guard here, and I'll go and make a call. No one leaves this carriage – not a single man, woman, or child! Got it?' the lieutenant barks. The conductor hears him, loud and clear.

The dishevelled, lax, somewhat tipsy fellow suddenly turns into a quick-witted, obliging public servant.

'Right. No one leaves. I'll see to it,' he says, nodding vigorously.

In the special operations room of the station, the lieutenant makes contact with his superiors.

'Comrade Captain! I'm reporting that Anadurdyeva was

76

taken off the train in Razdolsk at two a.m. and placed in an ambulance. It's about two hours away by rail handcar. Yes, there is, there is a handcar. And the passengers in the train carriage, what should we do with them? Detain them? Cordon it off? Organize security? Absolutely! Yes. I understand. The carriage is already uncoupled. It can be moved further away. Right, Comrade Captain. All clear.'

Ekaterininskaya Hospital is cordoned off by soldiers. Sentries are posted outside, and in the hospital grounds. Two figures in protective suits emerge from a door marked 'Morgue'.

Crowds of soldiers. All of them are freezing cold. Chaotic movement towards the gates, and away from the gates. A car drives out – after a document check, with special permission. At the exit, everything is doused with disinfectant.

In the wards the doctors are holding explanatory briefings for the benefit of the patients. One of the chiefs has seated the post-operative, ambulatory patients in a group, and tells them:

'Influenza is particularly dangerous to a weakened organism. All of you who have undergone surgery are highly susceptible to it. In order to avoid an epidemic, we must observe intensified safety measures. We will distribute masks and ask you not to go out into the corridor without them. You are expected to limit contact with others, insofar as possible. Go out into the corridor only if it is strictly necessary. The cafeteria will be off limits to you; the orderlies will bring you your meals in the wards. One more thing: at the first sign of illness or discomfort, please alert the medical staff immediately. Like the rest of the staff, I am also in quarantine. This means I will always be present somewhere on the ward,' the doctor says, in conclusion.

'Vasily Andreevich,' a youngish lad says, 'they were going to discharge me tomorrow. Does this mean I won't be able to go home?'

'They won't discharge you tomorrow, Kostin. And if you get too down in the mouth, I'll have to do another appendectomy on you,' says the doctor jauntily.

'Oh, anything but that! I'll just hang on for a bit then,' says the young fellow, smiling.

Sorin on the phone. He's talking to Sikorsky.

'His condition is critical, Lev Alexandrovich. He hasn't regained consciousness.'

Sorin walks up to Maier. Maier is coughing. Sorin wipes away the blood, props him up slightly higher, and goes back to the phone.

'Pulmonary bleeding.'

'Alexander Matveevich! Your wife is here with me. She wishes to speak to you.'

Sorin freezes. His face is harsh.

'Please tell her that I am busy at the moment. Thank you, Lev Alexandrovich,' he says, and hangs up.

He notes down in Maier's medical history: '1 a.m.: Oedema of the lungs, haemorrhagic (illegible)'.

Tonya walks along the corridor and tries to exit onto a stairwell landing, but they won't let her out of the ward. She sits down on the floor next to the stairs. Here she will sit until the end, not saying another word.

Maier. Sunken eyes, lifeless, rigid expression. Sorin covers his face with the sheet.

Sorin is seized by a sudden bout of coughing. He draws some liquid into a syringe and injects it into his leg.

A burning campfire. The frozen soldiers have built it in the grounds of the hospital.

'Lev Alexandrovich!' Sikorsky's head nurse has come to report to him. 'The district physician from the emergency services, the one who was on duty yesterday, has been locked up in the linen cupboard. He's kicking up a terrible fuss . . . and the officer in charge won't issue orders to release him.'

'Ask Captain Solenov to come by, please.'

The captain enters.

'Have a seat, please. There's a matter we need to discuss,' Sikorsky says to Solenov.

He doesn't sit down. Sikorsky gets up.

'Yes, sir. What is it?' Solenov says officiously.

Subordination of rank exists, after all. And Sikorsky, as chief physician of the hospital, albeit a civilian, is still superior in rank to the captain.

'Who gave orders to lock the district physician in the linen cupboard?'

'I did, sir.'

'And where is the ambulance doctor, and the orderlies?' Sikorsky says.

'In the autoclave room, the doctor's sitting room on the second ward, and the shower room,' the captain says crisply.

'From now on, I ask that you not take it upon yourself to decide matters that fall under my jurisdiction. We had agreed that all those exposed to the disease would be held at Sokolinaya Gora, not here.'

'When I transported them here, there was no such agreement,' the military man says, trying to justify himself.

'Lyuba!' Sikorsky shouts. 'Please ask the district physician to come here.'

'But . . .' Solenov objects. 'He belongs to the most contagious group.'

'Precisely. And in a few hours, he may exhibit the first symptoms of illness. I ask you . . .' And Sikorsky gestures towards the door.

Passing Solenov in the doorway, Kossel enters. Sikorsky puts on a mask.

'I offer you my apologies, my colleague,' he says, bowing to Kossel. 'I'm Lev Alexandrovich Sikorsky, the chief doctor of this hospital.'

'Kossel, Sergei Iosifovich,' Kossel says, introducing himself. 'For God's sake, please explain what all this is about.'

Sikorsky hesitates, then says:

'Yesterday evening, my colleague, a patient diagnosed with double pneumonia, was brought to the hospital. The patient was from your district – from the Hotel Moscow.'

'Yes, I remember. Maier was his name,' Kossel says.

'An hour ago, he died of pneumonic plague.'

'Pneumonic plague?' Kossel says. 'So, it was—'

'That's right. During the early stages of the disease, when you examined him, pneumonic plague resembles pneumonia. The incubation period, as you know, is very short, two or three days. The first signs of illness usually appear within twenty-four hours. Fever, chills, nausea in some cases . . .'

'If I have understood you correctly, I am now in quarantine?' Kossel asks evenly.

'Yes,' Sikorsky says simply. 'Please tell me, is there anything I can do for you?'

'Allow me to call my wife,' Kossel says.

'Of course. But please, think carefully first about what you will say to her. As you understand, the word "plague" cannot be uttered.'

Kossel nods, and dials the number.

'Dina? I'm sorry I couldn't call you sooner, Dina. I was called in for an urgent consultation. No, I wasn't able to, Dina. I couldn't. What nonsense! What nonsense! Don't cry, I beg you. I'll return! Of course, I'll return, Dina!'

Maier's body, covered with a sheet, is lying on the examining table. Sorin has manoeuvred his desk into a position with his back to the body. Sorin is obviously ill, coughing and out of breath. He is writing a letter:

Dear Comrade Stalin!
    By the time this letter reaches you, I will no longer be among the living. I am dying of the plague, as

a doctor from Saratov just did – a man I isolated and took care of until the moment of his death. I hope that the epidemic will be stopped; and, if this proves possible, I will consider myself to have given my life for the Soviet people. My situation, that of a doomed man, gives me the right, it seems to me, to ask a personal favour of you. In July of 1937 my older brother, Sorin, Semyon Matveevich, head of construction at a mine in the Tula coalfields, was arrested. Throughout his entire life, my brother's impeccable revolutionary spirit was such that the accusations laid at his feet during his arrest are unthinkable. I would ask you to intervene personally in my brother's case.

Dr Goldin, the pathologist, enters the dining room, rubbing his hands together. The table is set for only one person.

'Did Sophia Isakovna call, Nastya?'

'Yes, she's not coming home for dinner. She's at a conference,' Nastya says laconically.

'I see. As usual,' Goldin says, sitting on the chair with the high back without touching it, and unfolding his napkin. Nastya pours soup from a tureen and leaves the room. Goldin is just lifting the spoon to his mouth when the telephone rings.

'Nastya! Answer the phone, please!' Goldin says.

Nastya enters:

'That was the Commissariat of Health. You are urgently needed. They've sent a car.'

Goldin lays down his spoon.

'This is why I love my patients, Nastya. In contrast to the higher-ups, they never disturb my meals and are always prepared to wait a little.'

Goldin, at the reception desk of the Commissariat.

'. . . and now an autopsy is mandatory,' the Commissar is saying.

'Well, well . . . that's my job, but I fail to understand why the matter is so urgent,' Goldin says calmly. The Commissar raises his eyebrows.

'We have a strong suspicion that the patient died of the plague. We must confirm the diagnosis immediately. Three people were confined in accident and emergency, and one has already died . . .' the Commissar says.

'If it's really the plague, I assume that the others' prospects are very dim . . . I am prepared to do an autopsy, or two, or three, however many are required. But on one condition.'

'What might that be?' the Commissar says with faint irritation.

'Do you have confidence, Yakov Stepanovich, in my professional expertise?'

The Commissar waves his hand.

'Need you even ask, Ilya Mikhailovich?'

'Then I will perform the autopsy, observing all the precautionary measures – wearing a protective suit, a mask, following all the required procedures – provided you can guarantee that I will not be subject to quarantine afterwards. That is my condition.'

'Very well, Ilya Mikhailovich. I give you my word,' the Commissar says.

Anna, carrying her suitcase, tries to enter the Hotel Moscow. The entrance is guarded by a soldier in a sheepskin coat. He stands in the place of the doorman.

'We're full up, young lady, we're full up,' he says amiably.

'But my husband is staying here, we agreed that I would join him.' Anna is about to reach for the door, but the smiling young fellow fends her off abruptly.

'No entry. It's off limits.'

'But how will I find him, where will I look? I know he's here in this hotel!' Anna says stubbornly, with conviction. 'I'm from another city.'

'Well, wait here for a moment,' the man in the uniform says. 'What is your husband's name?'

'Maier, Rudolf Ivanovich,' Anna says, smiling gratefully at him.

The soldier leaves, locking the door from the inside.

On the lower floor of the hotel, a semi-basement area, two officials are talking to Anna – none too politely.

'No, young lady, you aren't asking the questions here. We are,' a man with a moustache says, turning her passport over and over in his hands. Jabbing the table with a finger, he says, in a sermonizing manner:

'So, you said you were his wife. That's not indicated in your passport. Now tell me, when was the last time you saw your so-called husband?'

'Just before he left to come here,' Anna says confidently.

The officials exchange glances.

'When was that, exactly?' Moustache says.

'Three days ago, I guess.'

'Wait in the corridor, please,' Moustache says. Anna goes out to the corridor and sits down in a chair.

One of the officials makes a phone call.

'Captain Gribanov here. Yes. Anna Kilim has been detained here. She was exposed three days before her departure. Yes. Very good, Comrade Lieutenant.'

*

Gribanov calls Anna back into the room, drums on the table with his fingers, and says, confidingly:

'Listen, young lady, your husband is having a bit of trouble at the moment. You'll have to stay here for half an hour or so.'

'What has happened?' Anna says, trembling in alarm.

'You'll find out all you need to know in good time. For now, you just have to wait. Sit here, in this room.'

'But may I see him?' Anna says, and dully repeats her request several times, though she knows they won't let her.

'No. It's out of the question. And I assure you, if you are too insistent, it will make your own life that much more difficult. Do you understand me?' Moustache says, smiling enigmatically.

He leaves the room, locking the door behind him.

Anna is left alone in the room. She makes a phone call.

'Lora Ivanovna! This is Anna. I arrived here today, but I can't manage to find Rudy. What's happened to him? Did he call when he got here? And he didn't call back? I'm calling from the hotel. They've detained me here and told me just to wait. I'll call you later. We'll come by, of course. Uspensky Lane? Well, Rudy will know. Yes, yes. Thank you.'

*

Fedor Vasilievich, a serious-looking official in uniform, is sitting in his office. Olya, his secretary, walks in.

'Fedor Vasilievich, the Zhurkin woman has arrived . . . you know, they called about her. They want you to talk to her.'

Fedor Vasilievich nods and says:

'Olya, find out which list Zhurkin is on.'

Olya looks through the pages.

'The second list, Fedor Vasilievich.'

'Good, ask her in.' The official nods. Ida Zhurkin, slender, pale, with shadows under her shining eyes, enters the office. Her bearing is upright, her manner frank and dignified.

'Good day. My name is Zhurkin. Zhurkin is my husband's surname. My father – believe me, I have never boasted of it in this way – my father was Grigory Solyus. Have you heard that name?'

The official raises his eyebrows in surprise. He jumps to his feet, smiling:

'Not only have I heard his name – I remember your father perfectly. I recall his funeral. How could I fail to remember? At the Novodevichy Cemetery . . . excuse me, what is your name, please?'

'Ida Grigorievna Zhurkin. I am here to ask for your help,' Ida says directly, and without a trace of servility. This makes her appear even paler and more attractive.

'Anything we can do, if it's within our power, Ida Grigorievna, of course,' Fedor Vasilievich says sincerely.

'Last night, your colleagues came to take away my husband, Alexei Ivanovich Zhurkin,' Ida says, almost regally.

'Yes, I'm aware of that,' Fedor Vasilievich replies mildly.

'At first I was stunned. I was certain that there was some sort of mistake, a misunderstanding . . .'

'Ida Grigorievna!' Fedor Vasilievich says, interrupting her. But Ida takes no notice.

'They took Alexei Ivanovich away, and I was left alone. And I began going over our lives, minute by minute, our whole life together.'

'Ida Grigorievna,' Fedor Vasilievich says, trying to stop her again. 'Let us postpone our discussion for a few more days. I'm very busy today.'

But Ida will not be deterred.

'But this is important! This is very important! I understand that I cannot deny my responsibility, I want to stress this. I accept my responsibility. However, looking over our past life, it is clear to me that there has been no mistake, no misunderstanding!'

'Ida Grigorievna,' Fedor says again gently, still trying to stop her.

'I realized that in burying himself in professional commitments he neglected the well-being of the Party, that he became insular, aloof; and the worst thing was that, in this way, he went over to the enemy. And now I understand how this might have happened, how it might have begun.'

'Ida Grigorievna.' Fedor Vasilievich tries one more time to interrupt her. 'You are upset now, after a sleepless night. I suggest you go home and rest for a few days and think about things, then come to see me again.'

'No, Fedor Vasilievich, that's impossible. I simply cannot keep this to myself. It is my duty to the Party to tell you everything, immediately.'

'Fine,' he says, and presses a button.

The secretary comes in.

'Olya, take down a dictation, please,' he says. She nods and sits down at a small table by the door. Ida Grigorievna continues her narrative agitatedly:

'I met Alexei Ivanovich Zhurkin in 1928. He was from a family of kulaks, a well-to-do peasant family, but he carefully concealed his origins from everyone. I didn't know either, of course . . .'

Two figures in protective suits walk along the hotel corridor. A third shows them a door, and they enter. Anna jumps to her feet and screams.

'Quiet, now, calm down. Don't be afraid. There's nothing to be afraid of. We've come to take you with us.'

'What's the matter? What's happening? Where is Rudolf Ivanovich?' she says, pressing her hands to her chest, and trying to hold back tears. 'Are you arresting me? But why? I haven't done anything . . .'

They conduct her out of the room and lead her along the corridor.

Sorin takes a coat out of the wardrobe, throws it on the floor next to the desk. He lies down on it, curling up his legs. He coughs; his face is distorted in pain. He is suffering . . . On the examining table, covered with a sheet, lies Maier, as before.

The Petrovsky Gates. Ekaterininskaya Hospital. Snow-laced fretwork of the wrought-iron fence surrounding the hospital. Grounds buried in drifts and mounds of snow. Campfires burning. People mill around the fires. A car drives in, and several figures in protective suits pile out. They hurry over to a campfire. The outlines of objects are obscured with a blanket of snow. The campfire seems to burn inside a pit, melting the snow that surrounds it.

A freezing-cold man, with a bottle in one hand and a mug in the other, runs out of the morgue.

Others holler:

'You got it? Bring it here! To warm up with! Medicinal spirits, right?'

They crowd round. Two of them take off their gas masks and hit the bottle. They stand with their backs turned, but it's clear they're passing it round.

A fellow in a protective suit takes an empty bottle, throws a burning match into it, and holding it in a glove, raises it above his head. The bottle catches fire from the inside, and the fellow waves it above his head, singing a snatch of a folk tune. From the crowd, a second one joins in. They begin to dance, and the clumsy protective suits and gas masks flash and flicker in the darkness. Bonfire.

Sokolinaya Gora. Cordoned-off quarantine hospital. Isolation chambers leading into a corridor. Two women pull a wagon with a vat of porridge, small cubes of butter, and a big stack of aluminium bowls. Through the little windows of the isolation chambers, they deliver porridge with a slab of butter on top, and glasses of hospital coffee, splashing some of it around.

Familiar faces: members of the board, from the chairman to Zhurkin, all Maier's travelling companions, the chambermaid from the hotel, hotel guests. The old woman who stole the tall, fur-lined boots is eating with gusto. Her expression, the only one among all of them, is absolutely contented.

*

A provincial hospital. The chief physician's phone rings. He picks up the receiver.

'Hello?' His face suddenly changes, and he gets to his feet. 'Chief Physician Kazimov. Who? Anadurdyeva? Yes, I hear you. Hold the line,' Kazimov says, and shoots like a bullet out of the office.

'Egorova! Where's Egorova? Send in the head nurse to me at once!' he shouts. After a moment, a skinny elderly woman with a stern, attractive face runs in.

Kazimov springs into action.

'Elena Adrianovna! This is urgent! Patient Anadurdyeva – how is she?'

'Patient Anadurdyeva was admitted here at three a.m., transported by ambulance, complaining of sharp stomach cramps. She was given a pain reliever, and two hours later she was feeling better. She demanded that we release her. I got a receipt from her. Everything is in order, Nikolai Khamidovich.'

But Kazimov is already running to the telephone, calling out in his wake.

'Follow me!'

The nurse stands directly behind him.

'Patient Anadurdyeva discharged herself. What time?'

'Six in the morning,' the nurse whispers.

'Six in the morning,' Kazimov repeats. 'Yes. We will

disinfect. And what is the matter with this Anadurdyeva? Right. Consider it done.'

Sweating profusely, Kazimov falls into a chair, wipes his forehead, and turns to Nurse Egorova. 'Elena Adrianovna! That was a call from the NKVD. They demand that Anadurdyeva be isolated immediately, and that her ward be disinfected. She has' – he presses his lips together and fixes his gaze on his nurse – 'influenza. Well, do you understand the import of this, what this might mean?'

The quick-witted Elena Adrianovna shakes her head and says confidentially:

'I don't even try.'

Fedor Vasilievich is sitting in his office. The secretary answers a phone call in the reception hall, then reports to him in the office:

'Fedor Vasilievich! Pick up the phone. It's from Kazan!'

Fedor Vasilievich takes the receiver. There is a loud crackling at the other end. Fedor Vasilievich blurts out angrily:

'What's going on there, is this some practical joke? You'll go before the tribunal! Do you have any idea where she's carrying it? To Central Asia, that's where, damn it! To Central Asia!' He looks at his watch. 'I give you four hours! Is that clear? She must be isolated within four hours! That's final!'

A window at the Lefortovo Prison. A queue outside it. They are mostly women. They all carry packages and bundles in their arms. A cheerful old woman turns away from the window.

She smiles at the person standing behind her. This person is Vera Anatolievna, Esinsky's wife.

'They accepted it! They accepted all of it! He's here!' she says and goes on her way.

Vera Anatolievna is nearly unrecognizable. All her youth and vigour are gone, and she has changed from an attractive woman into a severe, sexless being, without memorable features or specific age.

She approaches the window.

'Please look up Esinsky, Konstantin Alexeevich.'

'No. Not here. Next.'

Vera turns away. The old woman who was successful in delivering her parcel offers her some cold comfort:

'You won't find him straight away. You have to let some time pass. You'll find him yet! We've been searching for our loved ones for half a year, and you think you'll find him just like that!'

A corridor in the hospital. Tonya Sorin is sitting on the floor. Next to her, squatting down, is Lev Alexandrovich Sikorsky.

'Nurse Sorin, why are you sitting here next to the stairs? Let's go to my office. You shouldn't be sitting here. Please come with me.'

Tonya stares into the distance with vacant eyes, not seeing anything, it seems. She answers, however, in a hollow voice:

'I killed him. I'm the one who killed him.'

'Nonsense, Nurse Sorin! Don't talk nonsense. Alexander Matveevich was doing what a doctor should. It's the only way a real doctor can possibly behave. Do you understand?'

'I killed him,' Tonya repeats. 'I just feel it . . .'

'Come, come, Nurse Sorin! Why are you sitting here alone on the cold floor?' He tries to raise her up, but she pushes him away.

'Go away, all of you!'

A young female orderly comes up to Sikorsky and takes him aside.

'No, she won't get up. We wanted to pick her up bodily – she fought us off tooth and nail. It's clear she's a little . . .' And points to her head.

A queue in a shop. Old women, younger women, one middle-aged man with a face like a duck.

'He crawled out of the well, and they tied him up, there and then,' an old woman says.

'Where would he have found a well? Here in Maslovka we don't have a single well, only water pumps!' her friend says.

'No, not that kind of well – I mean the kind underground, with water pipes and whatnot, the kind with an iron lid.'

'Ah, that kind; well, that's another kettle of fish,' the neighbour says.

'So they upped and grabbed him, and they found poison on him. And they took him away. The car drove right up to get him.'

'A spy,' a third woman says. 'A White Finn.'

'There's lots of them around these days,' another one, wearing a plaid headscarf, says.

'And wreckers. Saboteurs,' the old woman adds.

'There's a big difference. A spy is one thing and wreckers are another. They're not the same,' says a solidly built man, commanding their attention.

'That's nothing! By Savielov Station, the day before yesterday, in the middle of the night . . . black devils, with little faces that looked like Martians, scary, really scary, turned up . . . but they came in a car! And they took someone from the fourth floor. Just like that,' says a woman wearing a knitted cap with a headscarf on top of it.

'What's the big deal? So, they took someone away,' the man interjects. 'They deserved it. There's a case against them, that means. My wife also said that her friend saw them jump out of the car, wearing all black, or maybe it was green, I don't remember, and they were running. And they were in masks too. They say it's the plague, that's what,' the man says significantly.

The women are alarmed.

'What are you saying – the plague?! When was the last time the plague hit us! Back in the days of yore!'

'Cholera, probably!'

'Oh, cholera, just what we need!'

'It's the last thing we need, of course; but cholera happens in our day too. One of my sisters died of it.'

'It's not cholera, I'm telling you. It's the plague,' the duck-faced man says insistently.

Out of nowhere, a stranger wearing a civilian's beret appears, tugs at the man's sleeve, then pulls him along gently.

'What are you doing?' the man says, surprised.

'Let's step out for a minute,' the stranger says, very peaceably, but obstinately.

'I won't go, leave me alone! I'm standing in the queue here!'

But another man appears, bigger and brawnier, grabs

the man by the shoulder, and says, not at all peaceably:

'You're coming with us, Citizen.'

In a government office, the duck-faced man is sitting across from an official. He's crushing his cap in his hands. His coat is lying next to him on a chair. He's wearing a worn-out service jacket.

'In this particular case, we are looking for the source of the rumours that are being spread. That is why, Citizen Kvasnikov, you must remember the name of your wife's friend. Preferably sooner rather than later. Otherwise we'll have to send a car for your spouse, Maria Efimovna Kvasnikova,' the chief tells Kvasnikov in an even voice. Kvasnikov seems to catch his drift.

'Tokareva is her name. Tokareva, Nina Nikolaevna,' he recalls.

'Where does she work?' the officer says mildly.

'In a cafeteria. On Karetny,' Kvasnikov says glumly.

'There now. And you said you didn't know. You recalled everything,' the boss says, praising him.

Anadurdyeva walks through the city towards the station. There is a marketplace in front of the station. She stops by the gate, buys a pastry, and, seeking out a secluded place with her eyes, walks further in. By a market stand, she notices two Turkmens, no longer young, wearing thick *chapan*s and *papakha*s, traditional robes and hats. They're selling dried apricots and pomegranates. Andurdyeva, smiling, walks over to them. They greet her joyfully. The older man shakes her hand formally, and the second, a bit younger, smiles affably. They speak in Turkmen. The old man beckons to her to follow him and leads her into the weighing station. In the weighing station there is a middle-aged woman in a dirty white apron. The man turns to her.

'Lina!'

'What do you want, Dovran?' says the woman.

'Kinfolk have arrived. Let her stay with you for one night,' he says.

The woman raises her eyes to Anadurdyeva. But Anadurdyeva can speak for herself.

'Can you help me, please? I'm coming from Moscow, on my way home. I had an attack of illness of some sort on the train, and they took me to hospital. But it has all passed, I have no more pain now, and I need to go home. Tomorrow my uncle will be going there, and he and I can travel together. I just need a place to stay for one night,' she says, smiling.

'I have no room, but I'll take you next door to my sister's. All right?' says the woman. Anadurdyeva nods.

*

The corridor of a police station. Several women and a man are seated there. A woman comes out of a room, weeping.

'Well, what happened?' a woman sitting on a bench asks her.

'I had to make a statement. They told me to return in three days, and we'll begin a search.'

'Oh, goodness me, three days! That's such a long time to wait,' says another with sympathy. 'But maybe it's for the best. If he had been killed by gangsters or run over by a tram, they would have informed you immediately.'

A man enters the reception room of the police chief and greets him.

'Comrade Chief, my daughter has gone missing, and I wish to start a search,' the man says gloomily.

'Well, I'll be!' the policeman mumbles. 'People have been coming here for two days, non-stop, with the same story! Who have you lost?'

'My daughter. Sozonova, Tanya, twenty-one years old,' says the man.

'Tanya, Tanya . . . I need her full name!' the officer says testily.

'Tatiana Dmitrievna Sozonova. Year of birth, nineteen,' the man says.

'How long has she been missing?'

'She didn't return home after work two days ago, and I haven't seen her since,' the man says.

'Have you checked at her place of employment?'

'Of course. They just tell me she's not there.'

'Where does she work?'

'In the Hotel Moscow, as a chambermaid.'

The policeman clears his throat.

'Hmm, a curious place, this Hotel Moscow. People keep disappearing. But your daughter – maybe she's run off with a suitor, and, meanwhile, you're looking for her everywhere. Maybe you should be looking for her somewhere else, eh?' the policeman says suspiciously.

'No, she's a good girl, my daughter. We've lived alone together since her mother died six years ago. She doesn't give me any trouble. And she doesn't have any suitors,' the father says with a sigh.

'Well, all right then, write down your statement here,' the officer says, showing him to a desk. Then he goes to the door and asks:

'Is anyone else waiting out there?'

A woman with a tear-stained face walks in. Her lips are still trembling, and she looks like she's been crying for days on end.

'Have a seat, Citizen,' the policeman says, but she remains standing.

'Well, what's your story?' he says in a weary voice.

'My husband is missing,' the woman says, and tears roll down her cheek.

'Hmm,' says the policeman. 'Fourth such case in the past two days. Please, sit down. Don't worry. Husbands turn up eventually, more often than not.'

In the corridor at the police station, a new couple joins the others who are already waiting. One is a middle-aged woman, the other is younger, and pregnant. They are anxious and upset.

Vera Esinsky waits in the queue by the little window at the Taganka Prison. There are about ten people in front of her, and some behind. Distressed women with bundles, with bags. Vera is wearing a thick headscarf, and completely blends in with the crowd. Not a trace of her former beauty remains.

The smoking area in the medical school. Young doctors, students in their last year. They're smoking.

'It's clearly very dangerous . . .'

'Oh, come on. It's the twentieth century in Moscow in wintertime.'

'There are epidemics that occur most often in winter. The plague, for example – plague pathogens perish at higher temperatures. The epidemic is stronger in the winter.'

'Where did you get that idea? The plague, what nonsense.'

'Two hospitals are in quarantine – Ekaterininskaya Hospital and Sokolinaya Gora.'

'Why Ekaterininskaya? Sokolinaya makes sense, of course, it specializes in infectious diseases.'

'What do you mean, "why"? Sabotage, that's why! I can tell you, in strictest confidence, that they came to take Grigoriev away!'

'Hush!'

'How's that?'

'Who in the world is Grigoriev?'

'You don't know? He's our chief physician for infectious diseases.'

And a bit further away, by the wall, two people are exchanging thoughts of an intimate nature:

'So then I say, please, you'll be more comfortable here. And show her with my eyes that it really is more comfortable. There's a couch, and all that sort of thing . . .'

*

The accident and emergency department of Ekaterininskaya Hospital. There's a seal on the outside. A hand in a rubber glove rips the paper with the seal from the door. Three figures in protective suits enter the area. One of the three is taller than the others – large and rangy. This is the pathologist, Goldin, but his face is concealed under a mask. The other two follow behind him, rolling along an autopsy table. They glance around. There are dishes in the sink. On the table is a small mountain of empty syringes, a letter addressed to 'Comrade Stalin', and the beginning of a second letter, with only a few words visible: 'My dear little Tonya . . .' On the floor, beside the desk, his face buried in his coat, lies Dr Sorin. He is dead.

'Shall we take him to the dissecting room?' one of them says.

'No, of course not. We'll do the autopsy here. Prepare the table.'

Goldin opens a small suitcase containing his instruments.

'Is there another ordinary table in the nurses' room?'

One of them goes to find out. He returns.

'The same kind.'

The table is covered with paper from a roll, and the two in the protective suits lift Sorin's body from the floor and move it onto the table. Maier's body remains lying on the examining couch.

'Where's the third?'

'In the nurses' room. It's the barber.'

'Put him on the stretcher and bring him here.'

Goldin begins his harrowing task: he cuts Sorin's clothing off the body, then runs a scalpel through the sternum.

Several hours later Goldin and his assistants leave accident and emergency and enter the anteroom, where a nurse and an orderly meet them. They begin to undress them one by one, removing their aprons, gloves, and masks, and dropping them into a sanitizer. The process is lengthy and finicky. Finally, Goldin goes out into the corridor, where a doctor from the Commissariat, who is clutching some papers, meets him. These are diagnoses, which Goldin must sign.

'Well, Ilya Mikhailovich?' the Commissariat doctor says.

'Classic case of pneumonic plague. One hundred per cent mortality rate. An extremely short period of illness, though. This is rather uncharacteristic for our situation. These forms usually appear at the height of the epidemic.'

'Sign here, please,' the Commissariat doctor says, and pushes the paper towards Goldin. Goldin signs. The outlines of two unassuming figures separate themselves from the wall and follow Goldin down the corridor. When Goldin is walking past a door with an inscription that reads 'Dressing Station', one of the unassuming figures jumps in front of him and opens the door, and the second figure, with an artful movement of the shoulder, presses Goldin in through the half-open door. And locks it.

Goldin's face expresses instantaneous indignation.

'Open up!' he shouts, pounding the door with his fist. 'Open up, damn it!'

The enraged Goldin kicks the door violently. The door shudders. He goes over to the window – snow-laden trees have bent over, nearly touching the glass. Just then, the door opens slightly, and a hand with a glass of tea appears through the crack. Goldin turns round – and bursts out laughing.

'Bastards!'

He takes the tea and puts it on the table, then goes over to the door and says:

'Hey, who's there? Open up!'

And, quite unexpectedly, a voice says:

'We received instructions to isolate you.'

'I see,' Goldin replies. 'I see. Well, be forewarned that I'm now going to break down the door; so, get out of the way.'

Goldin takes some sort of instrument from a cupboard, with which he jemmies the lock.

Tonya Sorin is still sitting on the stairs. Another nurse, her friend, is sitting beside her.

'Tonya, please have something to eat. Come on, why are you still here, Tonya? Let me put you to bed. I'll give you a little injection that will help you sleep. Just for a bit. How about it, Tonya?'

Tonya sits rigid, unmoving. Silent.

A briefing with the High Personage. Fedor Vasilievich, the senior official in charge, delivers the report.

'Thus, within the space of three days and nights, according to the protocol for Highly Contagious Diseases, we have identified eighty-three people: thirteen train passengers, thirty-eight from the hotel, and forty-two from . . . from the Commissariat board . . .'

'Was everyone detained?' the High Personage asks.

'One woman was never located.'

'I assumed you worked more efficiently than that. We don't need shoddy labour.'

Telephones ring, pens scribble, typewriters bang out numbers and letters of the alphabet. Aeroplanes fly, people toil and toil. On the table is a pile of photographs. These are photographs blown up to mammoth proportions, clearly taken from some sort of document. Anadurdyeva. Her portrait is passed round and laid out on all the desks.

A nurse goes up to Sikorsky and whispers something to him.

'What!' he says in astonishment. 'Impossible!'

Sikorsky runs down the corridor. Two figures stand by the door, apparently waiting for the door to fall down into their arms. There are loud bangs, scraping sounds.

'What's going on here?' Sikorsky barks at the guards standing by the door.

'Special instructions,' one of them says blandly.

'What on earth are you talking about?' Sikorsky bellows.

'Call the board,' the other says.

'Move away from the door! Where's the key?' Sikorsky says.

'We don't answer to you,' a guard says.

'I'm the boss here! I am!' Sikorsky yells. 'Move away from the door, I say!'

The two guards shuffle around a bit, then move aside. The door sways on its hinges, and starts to topple onto Sikorsky. He manages to prop it up.

'Ilya Mikhailovich! My dear man! Forgive me, for the love of God! I had no idea that such an outrage was happening! I beg you! Please!' Sikorsky leans the door against the wall, takes Goldin by the arm, and leads him to his office.

In the office.

'For three days and nights, Ilya Mikhailovich, people have shown themselves to be extraordinarily idiosyncratic. Yes, idiosyncratic . . . still, the staff is very good.'

'Will you allow me to contact the Commissariat?' Goldin says.

'Yes, by all means!' Sikorsky gestures towards the phone. Goldin dials the number.

'Good day, Yakov Stepanovich. I finished the three autopsies. I confirmed the diagnosis. The microbiological analysis will be ready in a few hours. Yakov Stepanovich! After the autopsy, I was detained, and they tried to put me in quarantine. Is the word of the Commissar of Health really so inconsequential?'

The Commissar is embarrassed.

'Believe me, Ilya Mikhailovich, those were not my instructions. I didn't have the slightest thing to do with it. You see, we charged another organization with responsibility for enforcing the quarantine measures.'

The telephone on the desk of the Commissar's secretary

rings. She flies into his office and makes a sign for him to pick up the other receiver. It's urgent.

'I'm sorry, Ilya Mikhailovich, one moment please!' The Commissar answers the other call.

'Yes. Yes. Well, well. Fine. Wait please,' he says, and immediately begins speaking to Goldin again.

'Ilya Mikhailovich, I've just received a call from Pervaya Gradskaya Hospital. A patient there died an hour ago. They suspect it's the plague. The clinical presentation is inconclusive. Please carry out one more autopsy, if you will. Unfortunately, if another case of the plague is confirmed, we will have to close Pervaya Gradskaya as well . . . they've sent a car for you.'

Two NKVD operatives, one Turkmen, another Russian, standing by the wall of a white clay house. They enter. A sweet, nearly full-grown girl greets them. The Turkmen enquires about her mother. The girl shakes her head.

'Mother is in Moscow,' she answers in her language.

The Turkmen translates into Russian: 'She hasn't come home yet.'

'Ask her when she expects her home,' the Russian says.

But the girl understands Russian perfectly.

'Today or tomorrow. Soon. We're waiting for her,' she says.

The men leave.

'I'm going to the station to get in touch with Ashkhabad. You stay here, Fazil. Keep watch. As soon as she gets here, call the station right away. I'll send a car. Someone will come to relieve you in twenty-four hours. Don't expect anyone before that,' the Russian, who is senior in rank, instructs his subordinate.

'Piotr Borisovich, maybe I could stay in their house? None of the locals would suspect anything. It's quite common for a guest from the city to stay overnight,' the Turkmen says cautiously.

'No, Fazil. Don't do that. Better just man your post. She'll come home, take fright, and run off. Then we'll have to go searching through the desert for her.'

The morgue. A figure in a protective suit in the corridor. Goldin is coming out of the dissecting room. Someone removes his protective suit. He washes, dries off his hands. He dials a number on the phone.

'Yes, Goldin speaking. No, I'm calling from the Pervaya Gradskaya. I performed an autopsy. Please be informed that it was a false alarm. Typical post-operative septicaemia. I'm sorry, but this is simply a medical blunder. The surgeons should wash their hands better and sterilize their instruments! No signs of the plague whatsoever.'

Piotr Borisovich reports to NKVD officer Fedor Vasilievich over the short-wave:

'No, she's still missing. She's not on a train.'

'What do you mean, not on a train?'

'I guarantee it. She's not there. I personally searched both of the only trains she might have been on. Looked every single passenger in the eye. She's not on a train.'

'Well, how about in Razdolsk?'

'After leaving the hospital she didn't check into the local hotel. She wasn't at the station. The last time she was seen was at the marketplace. It's like she disappeared into thin air.'

'What about the *aul*, the local village?'

'Not a trace of her. They say she hasn't come back from Moscow yet.'

Fedor Vasilievich, glowering, smacks the table with his palm, and adds:

'Remember one thing, Borodachev. If she doesn't materialize again out of thin air, this will be our last case. The very last. Is that clear?'

Fedor Vasilievich drops his head in his hands, then sighs; sighs deeply once more, and starts gasping for air. He throws himself back in the chair, and clutches spasmodically at his left shoulder with both hands.

*

Meeting at the Commissariat. An infectious disease specialist, Grigoriev's deputy, is delivering a report.

'Today is the fifth day of quarantine. If, after eighteen hours, no more signs of illness are observed in those who have been isolated, we may consider the danger of an epidemic to have passed.'

In a narrow kitchen, the woman of the house, two men, and Anadurdyeva are sitting at table. It is a touchingly simple meal: sauerkraut, pickles, potatoes, pomegranates, dried apricots, dried meat, and Turkmen flatbread.

'I lived in Russia for a whole year, studying at college, but then I dropped out. I was called home to get married. I've been in Moscow four times. I know everything there – the Kremlin, the Mausoleum . . .' Anadurdyeva is saying.

'And I haven't been there a single time, that's how foolish I am. It's less than twenty-four hours away; but I can't make up my mind to go,' the other woman says wistfully.

'I'm sending my son to Moscow to study, he'll be a scientist,' the guest says.

'How many children do you have?' the woman of the house asks.

'Six, so far,' the guest says, smiling.

'Oh, who did you leave them with when you left home?' the woman says.

'My mother is there, and my eldest daughter,' Ana-durdyeva says.

'How old is your daughter?'

'Twelve.'

'My, my! I have two, and I rush home from work every day, thinking they may have burned the house down! But you're so calm – leaving all your little ones behind! With a twelve-year-old!' the woman says, surprised.

'Not all. I brought the littlest along with me,' the guest says, and folds her hands over her belly.

Nastya is serving lunch. Goldin enters the dining room. His wife looks at him searchingly:

'Ilya, you look utterly drained,' she says, shaking her head.

'I'm getting old, Sonya,' he says with a grin. 'I haven't slept for two days. I'm falling down on my feet. I have to admit, I used to have more endurance.'

'I would never have guessed in a million years just by looking at you!' Sonya smiles wryly.

The telephone rings, and she gets up to answer it. Goldin calls after her:

'Sonya, don't ask me to come to the phone.'

He sits in his chair. His eyes are half-closed. The hand holding his spoon drops down next to his plate. His face shows two-day stubble.

Sonya, talking in the corridor, is standing up for her husband.

'No, no, that's out of the question. He has been working for the past forty-eight hours. He has just got home, and he's already asleep. No, I won't wake him up. Well, as you wish. But no sooner than in three hours!'

Sonya, now in quite a temper, goes into the dining room, saying:

'Just imagine!' But she sees that her husband has nodded off at the table, and simply shakes her head.

Telephones ring, people with papers run from one floor to another. Before the High Personage, his adviser bows, saying:

'Your order has been carried out. There are no more new patients. The General Secretary may be informed that the epidemic has been averted. The quarantine may be lifted.'

The High Personage nods:

'Lift it!'

The gates of Sokolinaya Gora Hospital. Dozens of people are pouring out of the gates. It's a sunny day. The passengers from the train exit the gates. Not recognizing each other in the crowd, the old woman in the tall, fur-lined boots, Ludmila Ignatievna, Sverbeev and Kulkov, all disperse in different directions. The members of the board are walking together. Grigoriev is chatting with Esinsky, who tells him:

'You know, they took me from Moscow Station, in Leningrad. I can just imagine what my wife is thinking.'

'They took me directly from home. But . . . my wife no doubt suspected the same thing,' says Grigoriev.

The chambermaids from the hotel, the guests, people who know each other, and people who are complete strangers, all walk through the gates.

By the gates of the hospital stands a lone Black Maria. These gloomy vehicles have already ceased to stir unpleasant associations in us when we see them.* Two figures get out of the menacing vehicle, cut into the crowd, and make a beeline towards a person wearing a coat with a lambskin collar.

'Alexei Ivanovich Zhurkin?'

'Yes,' Zhurkin replies flatly.

---

* Editor's note: 'These gloomy vehicles have already ceased to stir unpleasant associations in us when we see them'. This sentence, though stylistically problematic since it signals an abrupt shift in perspective, is important. This manuscript was written in 1988, the era of *glasnost* (openness) and *perestroika* (reform), not 1978, as Ulitskaya thought when she first discovered it (see afterword on p. 120). Here, in the spirit of that era, she is reminding her readers not to forget: to remember history, and to be aware of the suppression of history.

'If you don't mind,' one of the operatives says mildly, 'we'd like to have a little chat with you.'

The crowd around Zhurkin and the two figures seem to melt away, and he walks to the car along a path that suddenly opens up before him.

A time of kisses, reunions. The missing daughter is found, Esinsky sees his wife again, her head now grey. Anna Kilim leaves through the gates, and Lora Ivanovna, Maier's sister, rushes towards her. They embrace, and weep, saying his name again and again . . . Rudy, Rudy! The Grigorievs kiss. Many happy faces.

All the characters of this story, whether acquainted, or still strangers to one other, walk through the gates of the hospital together. In the background, the jaunty, cheerful sounds of a Soviet march can be heard: 'Broad is my native land!' And so on, and so forth . . .

At the Kossel home. Kossel's wife is sitting in her armchair. The portrait of her son is lying on the table in front of her. She covers her face with her hand.

'Sergei? I thought you weren't going to come back, either. Where were you, Sergei?' For the first time her eyes are focused and attentive.

'Dina, it was the plague. It was just the plague!' Kossel says. He smiles and takes his wife's dry, warm hand between his palms.

'Just the plague?' she asks.

He nods.

'Ah, and I thought . . .'

Now the march reaches a crescendo. And the day is marvellous and sunny. Festive, like a holiday. And, truly, it is a holiday. Old women are coming out of the church in Briusov Lane, greeting one another.

'Holiday blessings!'

'Merry Christmas!'

Through the wide-open doors of the church come strains of music, and the words 'The day of thy birth, Christ our Lord, illumined the world with the light of knowledge'.

All is drowned in the refrain of the glorious, cheerful march.

THE END

Afterword: Ludmila Ulitskaya
in conversation with Christina Links

Is your screenplay based on actual events?

I learned the story of these events, which were not widely known in the USSR, from my acquaintance Natasha Rapoport. Her father, a pathologist, played a part in the story, as it developed in Moscow in 1939. He was the doctor who examined the bodies of those who had died of the plague. There really were only three of them. The laboratory scientist who was trying to develop the anti-plague vaccine was infected during his experiments, and travelled to a conference in Moscow. The first symptoms of illness appeared on the evening of his arrival in Moscow; but prior to that, he gave a lecture at the conference and exposed a large number of people to the disease. Any one of them could have become a carrier of this plague. The NKVD (the secret police) was charged with tracking down all those who had been exposed, and the person who was given the responsibility to carry out the operation was Lavrentiy Beria, who was then the head of the NKVD. In those years, people had already grown used to the doorbell ringing in the dead of night, to disappearances and express trials carried out by the infamous *troika*s – insofar as it's possible to get used to such things, that is. Since everyone automatically assumed that arrest meant detention, deportation or execution, being detained merely 'for quarantine' felt like a gift from the gods. I was certain about the existence of the scientist, the proverbial 'virus from the broken test tube'; the doctor who isolated himself in quarantine with the first victim; and the hotel barber who had happened to come into contact with the scientist. The other characters sprang from my imagination.

As far as I know, the screenplay never became a film. Why?

There were almost no opportunities for a film to be made from it. The screenplay was written as part of an application to a film-making course, as an entrance test. I wanted to be admitted to the Moscow 'Higher Courses in Screenwriting and Directing', to study under Valery Fried. I sent the screenplay to Fried, and then we talked over the phone. He told me that he wouldn't accept me as a student. I wasn't even terribly disappointed – I hadn't really expected to be admitted on the basis of my screenplay – and then Fried added: 'There's nothing we can teach you. You already know it all.' And that is where my involvement in cinematography ended, for many years.

Valery Fried, although he believed I had done a professional job with the screenplay, would not in any case have recommended it to anyone. He had been incarcerated in Stalin's labour camps, and the idea that the NKVD had carried out at least one useful, 'humane' act was deeply disturbing to him. But the fact was that the NKVD really did manage to stop the epidemic, drawing on its rich resources and ample experience in arresting and 'liquidating' people. However surprising it may be, the security forces of the time proved to be stronger than the predatory force of nature. And this provides food for thought . . .

The screenplay is complex, and would be rather expensive to produce. I've hardly shown it to any directors, apart from Vladimir Mirzoev, who is a good friend of mine. But I don't know how to 'shop it around'. I wrote it, then put it aside. And now that the screenplay has been published in Russian, and in several other languages, I still haven't received any offers to turn it into a film. It seems to me, though, that it's just begging to become a television series. This is the biggest problem for the playwright – she makes a half-finished product, and the director is the one to bring it to fruition. This is, in fact, the reason I prefer writing prose, rather than plays and film scripts.

Did you change anything in the text before publication?
A few words, a comma here and there.

How was it possible, in the 1980s, to uncover the facts, to get the necessary information?
In those years, there was nowhere to get it from. Everything I

knew was based on that single conversation with the daughter of the pathologist I mentioned earlier. The other details were invented, including the happy *finale*, when the doors of the infectious diseases hospital, where all the people were quarantined, open wide, and everyone is set free.

At that time, all such information was classified; everything was restricted. Even today, no one knows about the cholera epidemic in Moscow, in 1959 – even though there are documents about it in the archives, and witnesses of the events are still alive.

Back then, the methods of the NKVD were different; but today too measures are taken that restrict people's freedom in Russia. Do you think the authorities' actions are appropriate to the present situation [the Covid-19 pandemic]?

Well, there wasn't any openness then, and there isn't any now, either. I would say that the present situation is more interesting – the authorities have been thrown into complete confusion. I don't know whether you have been paying attention to this topic, but, for the first time, the Kremlin has allowed the Russian regional governors to find their own independent solutions to the medical crisis, and to carry them out. And this is not openness; it reflects the helplessness of the authorities in the face of this crisis. The authorities need to impose drastic quarantine measures, which also gives them the opportunity to limit individual freedoms constitutionally guaranteed by the state. Does it not pose a threat to democracy when the authorities use a pandemic to restrict free-doms, and then decide not to return those freedoms, when the time comes?

In 1939, people were not told the truth about the potential epidemic in order to avoid panic. This was most likely justified, in part; but would withholding the truth for the same reason be considered justified today?

That's a difficult question. The great people of Russia – and I say this without a trace of irony – are used to the absence of truth. The truth is considered important by only a very small number of people – namely those who are able to think independently. And such people are always in the minority. For most people in Russia, the truth is considered to be a luxury. To a country that is used to the wholesale reign of lies, half-truths are very appealing.

How did your profession influence your choice of the subject of this screenplay?

In a formal sense, I parted ways with genetics in the late 1970s, though I never stopped being interested in it and feeling con-nected to it. To this day, there is nothing more interesting to me than this marvellous field of science, and the remarkable speed at which its mysterious laws are being revealed by researchers. I must admit that the subject is always present in my work, some-times at a very deep level.

Did you have other motives for turning to the subject of this book?

Somehow, a thought, not fully elaborated, had taken root in me – the thought that the plague was not the most terrible misfortune that could overtake humanity. Because an epidemic is a process of nature, potentially affecting not only people, but animals, too. But the epidemic of terror that is unleashed from time to time within human communities is 'man-made'; nature plays no part in the calamity, the evil, of political terror.

What interested you, touched you, disturbed you most of all about this event in 1939?

That it was a plague in the midst of another plague. In 1939, mass arrests had not yet ended. Thousands of people throughout the USSR were unable to sleep, trembling with apprehension that they might be arrested at any time. At that very moment, the threat of the actual plague, *Y. pestis*, emerged, an infection that originated in some laboratory . . . Does this sound familiar? Does it evoke any associations with the present?

As a geneticist by training and by vocation, how would you assess the response to the pandemic in Russia, and in the rest of the world?

The response has been varied, and there are two extremes. One view is that it isn't so terrible, that the illness is not even as serious as the flu. Not to worry . . . Another very common attitude is an alarmist one: it's our worst nightmare; it's the end of the world; it will lead to the demise of humanity. As a former biologist, I would suggest that the calamity will be overcome. The laws of such viruses suggest that the strain will weaken, and that the disease will grow less lethal. Moreover, no other infection has met with such a powerful and speedy scientific (as opposed to political) response.

The consequences of the pandemic are still unknown – perhaps it will mean a toughening of the power of the authorities. It will have effects, undoubtedly, but the effects are hard to predict. The influence of past pandemics did not encompass the whole planet. I hope that there will be transformation. I hope that funding for science and medicine will increase. I hope that the pandemic will level a blow to the current political system, which primarily expresses itself in selfish nationalism . . .

But the world will change in ways that are unpredictable. Humanity is facing a new trial – I hope it will not make us more closed-minded, more egocentric. I hope that we will realise that we live in one world, and that we need more compassion and love. And that will depend on us.